Sir John Harington

Twayne's English Authors Series

Arthur F. Kinney, Editor

University of Massachusetts, Amherst

TEAS 386

SIR JOHN HARINGTON
(1560–1612)
Photograph courtesy of the British Library

Sir John Harington

By D. H. Craig

University of Newcastle

Twayne Publishers • *Boston*

Sir John Harington

D. H. Craig

Copyright © 1985 by G. K. Hall & Company
All Rights Reserved
Published by Twayne Publishers
A Division of G. K. Hall & Company
70 Lincoln Street
Boston, Massachusetts 02111

Book Production by Elizabeth Todesco

Book Design by Barbara Anderson

Printed on permanent/durable acid-free
paper and bound in the United States of
America.

Library of Congress Cataloging in Publication Data

Craig, D. H.
    Sir John Harington.

    (Twayne's English authors series ; TEAS 386)
    Bibliography: p.
    Includes index.
    1. Harington, John, Sir, 1560–1612—Criticism and
interpretation.   2. Ariosto, Lodovico, 1474–1533.
Orlando furioso.   I. Title.   II. Series.
PR2285.C7 1985   828'.309   84–15807
ISBN 0–8057–6872–6

Contents

Editor's Statement

Drawing for the first time on unpublished Harington manuscripts and recent dissertations, D. H. Craig's comprehensive review of the life and work of Sir John Harington makes the first critical book devoted to him a challenging reappraisal of his accomplishment. If Harington is a jester at all, Craig argues, he is a jester in the sense popularized by Erasmus and More, as one who mocked only what is serious to highlight the seriousness of the mockery. His are jests that repeatedly "exploited the limits of the fastidiousness and the prudery of his time" to expose its hypocrisy and, much more seriously, the proclivity of man toward natural evil, which remains Harington's most abiding concern. His wide range of talents and achievements—in translations of Virgil, Ariosto, and the Psalms; in treatises on gambling, on the clergy, and on marriage; in epigrams modeled on Martial and satire modeled on Rabelais—led to a varied corpus unmatched by any other Elizabethan. We misjudge Harington, Craig argues, if we place the *Metamorphosis of Ajax* before the *Orlando Furioso,* and if we concentrate on his translated texts instead of the marginal commentaries they inspired. In just those margins where he lived, thought, and wrote, at the edge of greatness, he provides us still with "a windfall of unusual insights into Elizabethan and Jacobean England." This thorough yet provocative study is a seminal reevaluation of Harington that will be drawn on frequently itself in the years to come.

—Arthur F. Kinney

About the Author

D. H. Craig is a lecturer in the Department of English at the University of Newcastle, N.S.W., Australia. He was educated at the universities of Sydney and Oxford. He has published on Sir Philip Sidney and is presently working with a colleague on the Ben Jonson volume in the Critical Heritage series.

Preface

This book is a discussion of Sir John Harington's contributions to the culture of his time as well as an attempt to provide some measure of the lasting importance of his work. In the first chapter I survey his life, mainly from printed sources (the task of a full account, making wider use of manuscript material, awaits a future biographer). The next chapter considers Harington's main work as a translator and commentator—*Orlando Furioso in English Heroical Verse* (1591)—and a second work of this kind, still in manuscript, dealing with *Aeneid,* Book 6. Chapter 3 treats *The Metamorphosis of Ajax* (1596), Harington's main prose work (a long controversial pamphlet, perhaps best described as a mock encomium on the water closet). Harington's epigrams, written largely in the 1590s, are discussed in chapter 4. In chapter 5 a range of other works in verse and prose is considered: a verse translation of a medieval handbook of health and diet, which Harington called *The Englishman's Doctor* and published in 1607; a metrical paraphrase of the Book of Psalms, still in manuscript, dating from the years up to Harington's death in 1612; minor prose tracts on a biblical controversy concerning Elijah and on gambling, and major ones on the succession to Elizabeth I and the state of Ireland; and Harington's substantial supplement to a contemporary *Catalogue of Bishops,* in which he describes the characters and careers of bishops of the Church of England he had known or heard about.

I have tried to place these writings in the context of their antecedents in the varied forms they adopt and (where possible) to gauge something of the way they were received by their first readers. The student of Harington's life and works is fortunate in having an unusual abundance of contemporary materials to work on, and also in the growing number of books, dissertations, and editions by scholars since Harington's day that bear on them. I have indicated my indebtedness to these in my notes. A good deal remains to be done, not only on Harington's biography itself but also in identifying references to contemporary figures and events in his works—particularly in the satirical epigrams and in the *Metamorphosis*—and in locating and editing the letters and epigrams that remain unpublished. A systematic history of Harington's reputation as a writer and the use made of his work would be a rewarding study in itself: beginning with the puzzlement, admiration, and outrage of his contemporaries but including also stray items from our own century, such as Aldous Huxley's *Crome Yellow* (1921), which draws on *The Metamorphosis of Ajax,* and Anthony Powell's *Hearing Secret Harmonies* (1975), in which the hero reads and quotes from the episode of Astolfo's voyage to the moon in Harington's translation of *Orlando Furioso.* Such a history, however, is outside the scope of the present book.

In my opening, biographical chapter, extensive use is made of Harington's letters. They are perhaps the best-known of his writings, for their interest as sources for the period. As private communications with varied purposes, they defy any strictly literary analysis, and I have not attempted any. Even in considering Harington's work for a wider audience, the student has to come to terms with the fact that for a great deal of it, an exclusively literary treatment is not the right one. Harington's poetical art is often impure—homely, even amateurish—just as his efforts in prose are invariably personal and whimsical.

This book is the first (apart from editions) to be devoted entirely to Harington, and the first to look at his works as a whole. In my conclusion I give an estimate of Harington's place in the English literary Renaissance from this perspective. The problem that has presented itself throughout is the degree and kind of seriousness with which his works should be taken: his characteristic self-awareness as a writer—a mixture of self-consciousness and urbanity—makes this an unavoidable and perplexing issue. It is one of the aims of the book to argue that though Harington is never solemn, and though a great many of his literary gestures, like his efforts in the world of affairs, were misjudged, his achievement should indeed be taken seriously. He is best understood, it seems to me, as a follower of the great tradition of Humanist irony, of serious jesting.

In the quotations from manuscript sources below, I have expanded contractions, italicizing the added letters. In quotations from printed materials (with the exception of printed manuscript transcriptions), "i" and "j" and "u" and "v" have been regularized according to modern practice.

I should like to acknowledge gratefully the permission of Mr. A. R. Hill and of the County Archivist, Berkshire Record Office, to quote from the manuscript of Harington's *Aeneid* translation and commentary, Trumbull Additional MS 23; of the British Library, London, to quote from British Library Additional MS 27632, and to reproduce a detail of the frontispiece in one of their copies of Harington's Ariosto (pressmark C.70gl.); of the Bodleian Library, Oxford, to quote from Bodleian MS Douce 361, fols. 8–87; of the Folger Shakespeare Library, Washington, D.C., to quote from its manuscript of Harington's epigrams, Folger MS V. a. 249; of S. F. Vanni, Publishers and Booksellers, to quote from Allan Gilbert's translation of Ariosto; and of the Loeb Classical Library (Harvard University Press: William Heinemann Ltd.), to quote from Walter C. A. Ker's translation of Martial and H. R. Fairclough's translation of Virgil.

I have spent two periods in libraries in England and the United States working on Harington, one funded by a grant from the Australian Research Grants Scheme, the other on an Outside Studies Programme from the University of Newcastle. I have had generous assistance from the library staff at the Bodleian, British, Folger, and Huntington libraries, from the Berkshire Record Office, and from the University of Newcastle's Auchmuty Library. I should also like to thank Peter Beal, Elizabeth Story Donno, Christine Mangala Frost, David L. Frost, John Gillies, Marcus S. Goldman, Damian Grace, Phyllis Marie Hill, Emrys Jones, Peter Kuch, Kathleen M. Lea, M. H. M. MacKinnon, R. H. Miller, N. Frederick Nash, T. G. A. Nelson, Michael Orange, William A. Ringler, Jr., Kathryn Ronayne, and Gordon D. B. Walters for their help with this book.

D. H. Craig

University of Newcastle,
New South Wales,
Australia

Chronology

1592   Rebuked by Privy Council for employing printer's apprentice. Queen's visit to Kelston. High Sheriff of Somersetshire.

1594   Brings charges against Edward Rogers.

1595   Building of house at Kelston nearing completion.

1596   Publication of *A New Discourse of a Stale Subject, Called the Metamorphosis of Ajax*.

ca. 1597 Composes *A Treatise on Playe*.

1599   To Ireland with the Earl of Essex's expedition (April). Service in Connaught (May, June). Knighted by Essex (July). Battle of Curlew Mountains (August). Meets the Earl of Tyrone (October). Returns to England (November).

1601   Essex rebellion, execution of Essex (February).

1602   Death of Lady Rogers (January). Composes *A Tract on the Succession to the Crown*. Verses sent to James I of Scotland.

1603   Death of Elizabeth (March). Dedicates himself to serious studies and activities in "Farewell to his Muse." Imprisoned as a result of standing security for Thomas Markham (May–October).

1603?   Interview with James I.

1604   Star Chamber suit brought against him by Edward Rogers. Sir Griffin Markham implicated in Bye Plot and exiled for treason; Thomas Markham's debt cleared by Sir Griffin's forfeited lands. *Aeneid* 6 translation and commentary sent to Henry, Prince of Wales.

1605   Presents volume of epigrams to Prince Henry (June). Composes *A Short View of the State of Ireland* as application for the posts of Archbishop of Dublin and Lord Chancellor of Ireland.

1606   Attends Queen of Sheba masque at court.

1607   Publication of *The Englishmans Docter. Or the School of Salerne*. Revised edition of *Orlando Furioso*. Enters controversy with Bishop Joseph Hall over the marriage of clergy.

1608   Completes *A Supplie or Addicion to the Catalogue of Bishops to the Yeare 1608* and presents it to Prince Henry.

by 1612   Completes metrical paraphrase of the Psalms.

1612   Dies (November).

1615   *Epigrams* published.

1634   Third edition of *Orlando Furioso*. Fourth edition of *Epigrams*.

1653   *Supplie* published by his grandson John Chetwind as *A Briefe View of the State of the Church of England*.

Chapter One
Harington's Life and Times

In 1605, late in his career, Sir John Harington put himself forward for the posts of Lord Chancellor of Ireland and Archbishop of Dublin. He was, however, neither a lawyer nor a theologian. In his long letter of application he reviewed his life to date. Using the traditional metaphor of the world as a stage, and of men and women as players—some good for many different parts, he says, some only for dumb shows, some deserving applause, others only to be wept over—he summed up his own performances: "I playd my chyldes part happily, the schollar and students part to neglygently, the sowldyer and cowrtyer faythfully, the husband lovingly, the contryman not basely nor corruptly. Once I playd the foole to frendly. . . ." He wished now to act a Chancellor's part in holy fashion, so that he might not be deficient in his last role.[1]

He had indeed played many parts, in a life full of ambitious beginnings. Few of them led to unqualified successes; as a student, as he admits, he was negligent; however faithful as a soldier and courtier, and in spite of a strong family tie with Queen Elizabeth, he was never rewarded with profitable or powerful offices from the court; and he fared no better in his application for the posts in Ireland in King James's time. On the other hand, there were doubtless satisfactions in the roles he mentions of husband and countryman, in a loving family life and in the management of his estate and of local and county affairs.

His playing "the foole to frendly" probably refers to his having stood surety for a large debt of his uncle's, which had landed him in prison two years before when the uncle defaulted. Whatever the particular episode, Harington had certainly played the fool often enough in his time; he could rarely resist the temptation to take up the jester's bauble, which drew everyone's attention and licensed all sorts of satirical thrusts. For a courtier, this trait was no advantage. He himself anticipated that his readers would smile when they read his application for a chancellorship and an archbishopric; at a crucial time earlier in his career, his cousin warned him against his jesting, fearing that for all his valor and labor "that damnable uncoverd honestie will marr your fortunes."[2]

But the role he chooses not to mention on his list—that of poet and chronicler—was in the end his most important one. His own estimate of his success there was cautious, and he spoke ruefully of the scanty rewards he had had for his efforts.[3] Nevertheless, it is as poet, translator, commentator, and historian of his time that he has earned his fame. The fool's part, which stood in the way of his advancement in the world of affairs, contributed to the quality of witty display, of humorous frankness, which enlivens almost everything he wrote.

Family History

The background for Harington's varied career is in his family origins, immediate and more distant. He was born into an ancient and noble family, though his knighthood was not inherited but bestowed by the Earl of Essex in Ireland in 1599. The members of Sir John's branch of the Harington family achieved their greatest wealth as the result of their support for Edward IV and the Yorkist cause.[4] A Sir James Harington was richly rewarded for capturing Henry VI at the Battle of Hexham (1464). Calamity soon followed, however, and after fighting for Richard III at Bosworth Field in 1485 the chief representatives of the family were attainted for treason and their lands forfeited to the crown.

Matters of lineage were of great importance to the Elizabethan Sir John Harington, and to his father, also John Harington, since if they could prove their descent from the rich Yorkist Haringtons, and if those Harington lands, which had by then passed into the Stanley family, were to revert to the Crown, they might stand to regain the "twenty-five rich manors" lost at Bosworth Field. Proving descent was made difficult by the obscure origins of Sir John's grandfather Alexander. He was presumed to be a son of Sir James Harington, who was pardoned by Henry VII for his Yorkist activities and in due course became Dean of York, but this relationship was never firmly established. Neither Sir John nor his father succeeded in regaining any of the twenty-five manors.

Nevertheless, John Harington was able to leave his son a substantial estate and excellent connections at court. He had secured a post at the court of Henry VIII by about 1538; greater things were to come, for in 1546 or 1547 he married his first wife, known variously as Esther, Ethelreda, or Audrey (Sir John was the son of his second wife). Esther was described as the daughter of John Malte, the king's tailor, but she was in fact an illegitimate child of the king's. Sir John commented later that his father had had Henry's "good countenance, and a goodlie office in his courte, and also his goodlie Esther to wife." Esther brought with her estates in Somersetshire and Berkshire, spoils of the Dissolution of the Monasteries— some compensation, as Sir John says, for his ancestor's misfortune at Bosworth Field.[5]

At about the time that he married Esther, John Harington is mentioned as a confidential agent of Sir Thomas Seymour. Seymour, who was Admiral of the Fleet in Henry's reign, was made Lord High Admiral and member of the Privy Council on the accession of Edward VI; his brother, Edward Seymour, was made Lord Protector of the Realm. Harington testified on behalf of his master when Seymour was tried for treason, charged among other things with having made sexual advances to Princess Elizabeth while she was a member of his household. In 1549 Harington joined the admiral in the Tower. Seymour was executed; Harington remained in the Tower until April 1550. Something of his fervent loyalty to his disgraced master can be gathered from his son's note in his translation of *Orlando Furioso,* which describes how a week before his death in 1582 John Harington had written out the names of those still living from "the old Admiraltie"—those who had served Seymour. Though the noble admiral is long since gone, and his men are of all classes from knights to tradesmen, the note says,

yet the memorie of his service was such a band among them all of kindnesse as the best of them disdained not the poorest and the meaner had recourse to the greatest for their countenance and ayd in their honest causes. . . . (19.M)[6]

Harington's activities after his release from the Tower in 1550 seem to have involved the party of Lord John Grey; in 1554, at the time of the Grey uprising, he was arrested and imprisoned after some investigation by Bishop Stephen Gardiner. His imprisonment, according to his son's report, was "only for carrying of a letter to the Ladie Elizabeth, and professing to wish her well."[7] After Elizabeth's accession in 1558 Harington's involvement in momentous affairs of state ceased, though his association with Elizabeth did not: he continued to exchange gifts of jewelry and manuscripts with the queen, and was granted a number of offices.

Sir John's debt to his father extends beyond this material prosperity and this valuable set of influential connections. His father wrote poems and collected the poetry of his courtly contemporaries, in a remarkable miscellany his son continued, and which still survives.[8] While in the Tower in 1549–50, he translated Cicero's *De Amicitia* from a French version, and published it in 1550 as *The Booke of Freendeship*. He preceded his son in translating Ariosto: the passage on the fellowship of the "Admiraltie" in Sir John's *Orlando* was prompted by a stanza in the translation on the subject of friendship, which Harington proudly notes as his father's work. Elsewhere, Sir John says his father once wrote the tune for a song King Henry himself had sung, Harington senior having learned his music "in the fellowship of good Maister Tallis, when a young man."[9]

Among the poems of his own composition included in his poetic miscellany was "A sonnet made on Isabella Markhame, when I firste thought her fayer as she stood at the Princess's Windowe in goodlye Attyre, and talkede to dyvers in the Courte-Yard." The princess is Princess Elizabeth; Isabell Markham was one of her maids. Isabell's father, Sir John Markham, was Lieutenant of the Tower when Harington was imprisoned there in 1549. Two of the poems addressed to her are dated this year. Harington's first wife was alive as late at 1555; she bore him one daughter, Hester. She must have died sometime between 1555 and 1559, allowing Harington to marry Isabell in that year.

The Markhams of Cotham were a well-established county family from Nottinghamshire. They had served the crown and the counties of Nottinghamshire and Derby for generations; Isabell's father was knighted by Henry VIII at the siege of Tournay in 1513, and had been High Sheriff of the two counties as well as Lieutenant of the Tower. In Mary's reign, Isabell was banished from Elizabeth's household for her determined Protestant views, according to her son Sir John.[10] Two of her siblings, Thomas and Frances, married into recusant families. Sir John records an early memory of Thomas and Isabell quarreling at his parents' Stepney house over matters of religion: Thomas had brought Lord Hastings to dinner, and while prayers were saieng he walked out into the garden, which my mother taking ill, for she was ever zealous in her faith, said to hir brother Mr. Thomas Marckham . . . that if he brought guestes thither that scorned to pray with her, she would scorne they should eate with her.[11]

Sir John's affection and admiration for his mother are expressed in his *Orlando Furioso*. He says that he has rendered the death of Isabella in the poem "to the uttermost of my poore skill, of a speciall love and reverence I bare to the name, having had an *Isabell* to my mother" (29.M). He draws special attention to stanza 31 of his translation, which he says may stand as a prophecy of his mother's life and death: whoever bears the name Isabella, the poem says,

> Shal be both wise and continent and chast,
> Of faultlesse manners and of spotlesse fame;
> Let writers strive to make their glorie last
> And oft in prose and verse record the same;
> Let Hellicon, Pindus, Parnassus hill
> Sound *Isabella, Isabella* still.
>
> (29.31)

Isabell had continued to serve Elizabeth, as one of the ladies of her privy chamber, up to her death in 1579. The queen seems to have recognized that the two Haringtons had earned her special favor by their long and loyal service. Her gratitude extended into the next generation—to their son Sir John—and if, with the exception of his commission to serve in Ireland, it did not result in any substantial employment, it was nevertheless shown in the fact that she never failed to forgive him in the end for the series of indiscretions that punctuated his life as one of her courtiers.

Early Life and Education

At the time of the birth of their eldest son, John and Isabell Harington were living in London (a second son, Francis, was born two or three years later). The infant was christened John at Allhallows London Wall on 4 August 1560. Queen Elizabeth herself was godmother, and the Earl of Pembroke godfather.[12] As we have seen, one of the young John Harington's early memories is of a family quarrel in his parents' house and garden at Stepney; as late as 1565 his father is described as being "of London." By 1569, however, the family seems to have moved to Kelston Manor, in Somerset. The manor had belonged to Bath Priory. It was granted to John and Esther Malte in 1546 and came into John Harington's possession after his marriage to Esther. It lies on the River Avon about three miles from Bath, on one of the roads to Bristol. Collinson says that John Harington began a manor house there, which his son Sir John completed.[13]

By 1570 or thereabouts the young John Harington was at Eton. The vice-provost of the school was William Wickham, later to be Bishop of Winchester; Harington recalled that when the schoolmaster was away, Wickham would himself "dyrect the boyes for their exercises; of which my self was one, of whom he shewd as fatherly a care, as if he had bene a second tutor to me."[14] Another early memory of school is of Thomas Thomas, *praepositor* or prefect at Eton until he left for Cambridge in 1571, and in later life compiler of a popular Latin dictionary. "Come old friend *Tom*," says Harington in his satirical pamphlet, *The Metamorphosis of Ajax*, "you have made rods to jerke me withall ere now, I thinke I shall give you a jerke, if you do not helpe me to some English for this word."[15]

The provost at the time was William Day, later to succeed Wickham at the see of Winchester. Harington remembered his plain sermons and his tricks of pronunciation, as well as an incident that suggests that as a schoolboy Harington was already cast among the jesters: Day broke his leg after falling from his horse,

whereupon some waggish schollers, of which I thinke my selfe was in the *Quorum,* would say it was a just punishment, because the horse was given hym by a gentleman to place his sonne in Eaton, which at that tyme we thought had bene a kinde of sacriledge. . . .[16]

In the notes to *Orlando Furioso,* Harington recalls that his first task at school after learning to write Latin was to translate from Foxe's *Book of Martyrs* the story of Elizabeth's sufferings in the time of Queen Mary. The labor was undertaken with his fellow-scholars Thomas Arundell and Sir Edward Hoby, and the "litle booke" that resulted was given to Queen Elizabeth (45.H). From an epigram we learn that it was at Eton that Harington began to write poetry, to follow his "Sweet wanton Muse, that, in my greatest griefe, / Wast wont to bring me solace and reliefe" (no. 427).[17]

There is evidence, too, that the schoolboy kept up contacts with his parents' courtly circle. The queen was the recipient of the translation from Foxe; in 1575, she sent Harington a copy of her speech to Parliament expressing her determination not to marry. The speech came with a note from the queen addressed to "Boye Jacke" and telling him to ponder her words

in thy howres of leysure, and plaie wythe theme tyll they enter thyne understandinge; so shallt thou hereafter, perchance, fynde some goode frutes hereof when thy Godmother is oute of remembraunce; and I do thys, because thy father was readye to sarve and love us in trouble and thrall. [18]

While at Eton Harington was also in touch with Sir Walter Mildmay, Chancellor of the Exchequer, who sent him a small volume of his writings and sayings (*Orlando,* 22.M).

In 1576 the young John Harington left Eton for King's College, Cambridge. [19] Recollections of his life there are scattered through his writings. He remembered his tutor at King's, Samuel Fleming, as "a grave and learned man and one of a verie austere life"; Fleming read him Aristotle and Plato and instructed him carefully in Greek and Latin (*Orlando,* 14). He says that Dr. John Still, who examined him for the Bachelor of Arts degree he was granted in 1578,

was often content to grace my young exercises with his venerable presence, who from that time to this hath given me some helps, more hopes, all incouragements in my best studies. To whom I never came but I grew more religious. From whom I never went but I parted better instructed.

We hear, too, of Robert Bennet, later Bishop of Hereford, who as a Master of Arts "playd well at tennis" and as a Bachelor of Divinity "would toss an Argument in the Schooles better then a ball in the tennis Court." Dr. William Chaderton is recalled as "well beloved amonge the schollers, and the rather for he did not affect any sowre and austere fashion either in teaching or goverment as some use to do, but well tempered both with courage and curtesie." Dr. Bynge, Regius Professor of Civil Law, read Justinian with Harington in his final year. [20]

Among the incidents he recalls from his time at Cambridge is a learned debate on the question of whether the style of the Scriptures is barbarous, and another on "Whether Rhetoricall figures and tropes, and other artificiall ornaments of speach taken from prophane authors, as sentences, Adages, and such like, might be used in Sermons."[21] In attending to these disputations he was following the advice of William Cecil, Lord Burghley, who wrote to him in 1578 thanking him for his letters and recommending that he read Cicero, Livy, Caesar, Aristotle, and Plato, and, above all, attend lectures and disputations when they were held.[22]

In spite of all this earnest instruction, Harington confesses that he was "a truantly scholer" at Cambridge. A letter of 1580 suggests that he had been involved in a liaison that had alarmed his tutor and his family.[23] He records many memories of the convivial side of university life, like this scene at a commencement feast in the college dining hall:

when we have bene in the midst of some pleasant argument, suddenly the Bibler hath come, and with a lowd and audible voyce begunne with *Incipit libri Deuteronomium, caput vicesimum ter-tium.* And then suddenly we have bene all *st tacete,* and hearkened to the Scripture. . . .[24]

Equally vivid is the picture in the *Metamorphosis* of the theaters in Cambridge and their staff

that for feare least they should want companie to see their Comedies, go up and downe with vizers, and lights, puffing and thrusting & keeping out all men so precisely; till all the towne is drawne by this revell to the place; and at last, tag and rag, fresh men and subsizers, & all be packt in together, so thicke, as now is scant left roome for the Prologue, to come upon the stage. . . .[25]

In 1581, Harington took the Master of Arts degree and, in November of that year, entered Lincoln's Inn in London to study law. Though his stay there was short—his father died in July of the next year and he seems to have left the Inn then to enter into his inheritance[26]—the law made a lasting impression on him. In 1596, in the *Metamorphosis,* he confesses that his studies stopped part way through Littleton's *Treatise of Tenures,* and admits he is only a "punie" of Lincoln's Inn, but he champions the virtues of the Inn enthusiastically. Not only does it have a privy with a chimney for ventilation which "putteth downe all that have bene made afore it"; the Inn is in a flourishing state for (among other things) furnishing the realme with most honourable, upright and wel learned magistrates, great sergeants, grave counsellers, towardly barresters, yong gallants of worth and spirit *sans nombre*. . . .[27]

At the time of the *Metamorphosis,* then, Harington seemed to be happy to regard himself as "a Lincoln's Inn man"; he is, indeed, called so in *Ulysses upon Ajax,* a scurrilous rejoinder to his pamphlet.[28]

On 1 July 1582 Harington's father died in London,[29] and the young John Harington's studies came to an end. Other parts now awaited the happy child and negligent scholar: as husband, countryman, courtier, poet, soldier and, not least, as fool.

The 1580s:
Husband, Colonist, Translator, Playgoer

Harington, as the elder son, was heir to his father's property and came into possession in June 1583. It appears that in that summer, and into 1584, he was involved in a risky traffic in the books of the recusant Edmund Campion. His father had held a permit for carrying about Campion's books, and letters in the State Papers allege that James Baker, a servant of the young John Harington's and "a very rebellious papist," had been misusing the permit to distribute forbidden books from the Continent. Sir Matthew Arundell, a leading recusant and old friend of the Harington family, was alleged to be the sponsor of the distribution. Harington, it was suggested, had received some of the books from Arundell. The matter does not seem to have been taken any further.[30]

In the course of his career, Harington was several times accused of being a Papist. His reply was that he belonged to none of the three rival religions in England but was "a *protesting Catholicke Puritan.*" Like his parents, he was a loyal member of the reformed English Church, but his Protestantism was tempered by a respect for the traditions of the Old Faith—he once reminded his readers that England had, after all, been officially Catholic in their fathers' or grandfathers' time, under Mary.[31] He was less tolerant of the Puritans, and deplored what he saw as their hypocrisy and their dangerously destructive attacks on the established Church, throughout his life.

Harington involved himself in another politically sensitive issue in 1584: the question of the Bond of Association. The Bond, pro-

mulgated in 1584, established a council to protect the queen against
plots on her life and to deny the throne to any claimant and to the
heirs of any claimant in whose name a successful attempt was carried
out. The obvious heir to the throne in 1584 was the Catholic Mary
Queen of Scots; the Bond would have excluded James VI of Scotland,
her son, as well, in the case of any attempt on the throne made in
Mary's name. Loyal citizens were urged to sign copies of the Bond,
which were circulated through the country.[32] Harington later described its reception in Somerset, and the rumors that if the leading
men of the county did not sign they would offend Leicester and his
party and be condemned as members of "the Scottishe faction."
Harington says that he refused to sign the Bond, thinking it an
invention of the Puritans and "an engine of battery against the house
and title of Scotland."[33] Harington continued to make public his
support for James as a candidate for the succession to Elizabeth in
the years up to the queen's death.

In September 1583, shortly after coming into his inheritance,
Harington married Mary Rogers, daughter of his neighbor Sir George
Rogers. Sir George had died in 1582, but Mary's mother, Lady
Rogers, lived on until 1602.[34] Dozens of Harington's epigrams are
written for or about Mall (as he called his wife), and more than a
score refer to her mother; they suggest a lively but resilient marriage
on the one hand and a valued but uneasy relationship with his
mother-in-law on the other. They tell of Harington's frankly sensual
love for his wife, and her reciprocation (nos. 26, 390, 262). He
wants her to be restrained in dress, solemn in church, "as busie as
a Bee" in his house ("Having a sting for every one but mee") but
in bed to be "as wanton, toying as an Ape" (nos. 332, 299). In his
absence, Harington says, Mall's song is "Com home, sweet heart,
yow stay from home too long" (no. 382).

The Haringtons' eldest son, John, was born in 1589; there were
eleven children in all,[35] of whom two died at birth. In an epigram,
Harington calls the nine surviving children "Nine organpipes, our
loves assured pleadges" (no. 369).

Many of the epigrams addressed to Lady Rogers are jokes for her
amusement; there are also more barbed ones, recording domestic
incidents like a late dinner at Lady Rogers's house or a maid's
carelessness (nos. 39, 28) or expressing a grievance at Lady Rogers's
reproaches for his lustfulness or frequent absences (nos. 402, 369).
Lady Rogers's power over her son-in-law rested on the wealth she

was to leave to her heirs; according to one epigram, the power was bluntly exercised, and any unpleasing remarks were silenced with "peace, or else a thousand pound [lost]. . . . / Thus, wealth makes you command, hope me obay" (no. 97).

Harington's relations with his brother-in-law, Edward Rogers, also followed a stormy course. In 1586 they traveled together to Ireland as "undertakers" of the Munster plantation scheme.[36] The Earl of Desmond had died in rebellion against the English in 1583; a vast area in Munster, in the South of Ireland, had thus fallen in excheat to the crown. Plans to divide up the land among English settlers were finalized in 1586; "undertakers" of the scheme were to rent "seignories" or portions of land up to twelve thousand acres. The scheme was particularly recommended to the younger sons of gentlemen, being "fit for gentlemen of good behaviour and credit, and not for any man of inferior calling."[37] Harington says he spent a few months in Ireland on this occasion (*Orlando*, 10.H). Presumably he was one of the group of "undertakers" who, having received grants from the crown in June 1586, crossed to Ireland only to find that no arrangements for assigning lands to them had been made. After spending some time at coastal ports, they returned to England in the late summer or autumn of that year.[38]

The plantation had some years of success before the 1598 uprising, once lands had been assigned—Sir Walter Raleigh and Edmund Spenser were both "undertakers" on a considerable scale[39]—but there is no indication that Harington or his brother-in-law played any further part in the scheme. Some strain in the relations between the two men is suggested by the comment in an epigram to Lady Rogers that her son Edward is "too much like his mother" (no. 191). In any case, there was an open quarrel in 1593 and early 1594, and Harington brought charges against Rogers, alleging that he had threatened him as they were coming out of Westminster Hall together, and had boasted since that he pulled out a handful of hair from John Harington's beard; on another occasion, he says, Rogers and his man drew their swords and were about to set on him, though he was armed only with his rapier. The grounds for the quarrel seem to have been Lady Rogers's property, since Harington alleges that Rogers is reported as swearing that "he would die at the gates [of his mother's house] rather than the said John . . . should carry one rag out of the house." To Rogers's threat that he would have some disputed trees "out of his throat," Harington had replied " 'there grew none there.' "[40] After Lady Rogers's death in 1601, quarrels with Rogers were to bring Harington to the notice of the authorities once again.

Harington's main literary project between 1583 and 1591 was his translation of Ariosto's romance epic *Orlando Furioso*. His interest in the great Ferrarese poet may well have been aroused by his father, who (as many references in his poetic miscellany show)[41] was familiar with the *Orlando* and had (as we have seen) translated a stanza from the poem, which his son used in his own version. According to a traditional story, the project of making a complete translation was the queen's idea. In the version given by Thomas Park, Harington translated the scurrilous tale of Iocondo from canto 28 and his version circulated among the ladies at court. It fell into the hands of the queen, who sent immediately for the translator, "severely reprimanded him for endangering the morals of her maids of honour," and "ordered him to retire to his country-seat, and not appear in her presence till he could produce a complete version of the whole poem." In support of this story is Harington's comment on the translation in the preface of the *Metamorphosis:* "The whole worke being enjoyned me as a penance by that saint, nay rather goddesse, whose service I am only devoted unto."[42]

Whatever its origins, the *Orlando Furioso* was recognized by Harington's contemporaries as an important translation and was anthologized for the qualities of its verse.[43] It won Harington favorable notice throughout his career. In an epigram, he reports the Earl of Essex's approval and the book's wide circulation (no. 77); he found it had preceded him in Ireland when he returned there in 1599; he read from it to King James in 1603, and sent his son Prince Henry a copy. A second edition was published in 1607, with detailed revisions in the verse by the translator.[44]

Harington was proud of the illustrations in his *Orlando,* which were among the first copper engravings to appear in an English book, and were, he says, produced under his direction (*Orlando,* 17). This interest in the technical side of book production is curiously borne out by a letter from the Privy Council in May 1592, which rebukes Harington for having twice enticed an apprentice printer and engraver from his master's service to his own; such activities are improper for one of Harington's "quallity and calling," the letter says.[45]

Harington includes a great deal of biographical detail in the notes and the rest of the critical apparatus to the *Orlando,* and they have often been quoted in these pages. The reader learns there that Harington's interest in the visual arts goes beyond the illustrations to his book to painting and sculpture (what he calls "drawing and carving"); he says he takes pleasure in such works "as pleasing ornaments of a house and good remembraunces of our friends," and describes a sitting he attended in which the miniature-painter Nicholas Hilliard took a likeness of the queen "in white and blacke in four lynes only" (33.H).

The *Orlando* volume also gives evidence of Harington's interest in plays and the theater, to add to the theatrical metaphor in *A Short View* quoted at the beginning of this chapter and the picture of the bustle before the opening of a play in Cambridge. In Book 20, Astolfo and five other knights are trapped in the gladiatorial theater of the Amazons. As a last resort, Astolfo takes his magic horn and blows a blast, which has its usual effect of scattering all who hear it in terror. Combatants and spectators alike flee from the theater in confusion,

> As tumultes often are at stage playes bred
> When false reportes of sudden fires are heard
> Or when the overloden seates do cracke,
> One tumbling downe upon an others backe.
> (20.61)

The simile, with its vivid details of panic in a theater audience, is Harington's own.[46]

Harington seems to have had little regard for popular drama, such as interludes: he refers to them slightingly in his *Treatise on Playe,* calling their actors "illiberall, base, and ridiculous." Yet in the *Metamorphosis* the clown Richard Tarlton is remembered as an excellent comedian, and Harington recalls how one of Tarlton's satiric expressions was "admitted into the Theater with great applause."[47] It was academic drama that impressed Harington most, however. Defending the theater in his *Orlando,* he claims that there is profit as well as pleasure to be had from a play like Thomas Legge's *Richardus Tertius,* played at Cambridge in his time. The ghastly example of Richard, his murdering of members of his family, his "short and troublesome raigne," would impress even the tyrant

Phalaris, "and terrifie all tyrannous minded men from following their foolish ambitious humors." University comedies like *Pedantius* and *Bellum Grammaticale* are full of "harmeles myrth," he continues; and even in a London comedy like *A Game of Cards,* there is a great deal of "good matter, yea and matter of state" (9). A few years later, in the *Treatise on Playe,* Harington again defends plays, and especially tragedies, against the "presyser [puritanical] sort" who would ban them.[48]

An assortment of evidence suggests that Harington's interest in plays and the theater continued throughout his life. A list he compiled in about 1610 of the plays in his library survives in the Harington papers.[49] It includes fifteen by Shakespeare and others by Kyd, Lyly, Middleton, Marlowe, Jonson, Dekker, Fletcher, Marston, and Webster. Harington had collected a respectable proportion of all the plays printed in London between 1588 and 1600, and had a remarkably complete collection for the years 1600–1610.[50] In his commentary on Book 6 of the *Aeneid,* presented to Prince Henry in 1604, he includes a reference to Falstaff—even if it is, admittedly, a strikingly unsympathetic one: the soldiers Virgil shows in Hades are

swaggring companions that follow war owt of theyr humor, and lyve thearin disorderly & lycentiowsly lyke S*i*r John falstaffe, robbing men of theyr pay, and selling or fleesing theyr companyes, ravyshing women and soch lyke, and dye commonly w*i*th an oth in theyr mowths as Ariosto discrybeth Rodomont. . . .[51]

A late reference to the stage occurs in a letter of Harington's to Thomas Sutton in February 1610, where among the divine retributions visited on the head of Sir John Skinner is numbered the fact that "in his life tyme hee should bee playd uppon the stage soe extreme scornfully; which, I suppose, of all the rest did most breake his heart."[52]

Into the 1590s: Builder, Courtier, Satirist

As we have seen, Harington's father had moved to Kelston by 1569. It was left to his son to complete the house he had begun there. Already in the father's time it was said to be the largest in Somerset.[53] The house the two Haringtons built was demolished in the eighteenth century, but fortunately a description of it by Bishop

Richard Pococke, who visited Kelston in 1764 during the demo-
lition, survives. It was of stone, Pococke says, with two towers,
mainly of brick. The doorways had doorcases with classical details;
inside were two grand rooms, each with an elaborate chimney-
piece.[54] One of the chimney-pieces with a bas-relief, apparently
depicting the exaltation of Joseph by the Pharaoh, survives.[55]

Collinson says that the house was "erected in 1587 . . . after a
plan of that celebrated architect James Barozzi, of Vignola."[56] This
is unlikely, though it may be that one or more of the designs for
the decorative features of the house were taken from Vignola's book
on the five orders of architecture.[57]

One aspect of the Kelston house achieved fame in its own time:
its fountain. In a letter printed in Harington's *Metamorphosis,* "Philostilpnos" (identified by Donno as Edward Sheldon, who married
a Markham cousin of Harington's) mentions among the things at
Kelston he has heard "much boasted of" and is keenest to see "a
fountaine standing on pillers, like that in Ariosto, under which you
may dyne & suppe."[58] In Collinson's *History of Somerset* there is an
engraving of the fountain. Water flows out of a barrel into a bowl
and then into a square basin, which is raised off the ground on four
columns.[59] The fountain in Ariosto is in *Orlando Furioso,* Book 42.
Harington's translation is abbreviated but adds a detail not in Ariosto,
the marble vessel, which

> . . . tooke the water from the azure skye
> From whence with turning of some cock or vice
> Great store of water would mount up on hye
> And wet all that same court ev'n in a trice.
>
> (42.75)

Ariosto does not mention the characters dining under the fountain,
as Harington does (42.71).[60] Townsend Rich suggested that the
"cock or vice" in the fountain of Harington's translation is the
forerunner of the plumbing arrangements of his water closet invention. Margaret Trotter has pointed to the similarities between the
modified fountain in Harington's *Orlando* and the fountain at Kelston
illustrated in Collinson.[61] Perhaps Sir John changed the fountain of
Orlando to match the fountain his father had built (Collinson's engraving shows a date of 1567 on the fountain), or perhaps the
fountain in *Orlando* inspired in Sir John a feat of garden plumbing

in constructing one to match (if the date in Collinson is an error). Whichever was the case, the story of the two fountains combines intriguingly Harington's activities as a translator and his interests in plumbing and building.

The building work at Kelston was lengthy and expensive. Sir John's resources were large, but not unlimited: according to an assessment made in 1589, he was in the second rank of the wealthy residents of Somerset.[62] In a letter of 1595, Sir John complains that the house is nearly finished, but not nearly paid for.[63] There is a rueful comment on his building ambitions in an epigram of 1603, where he offers his advice to the new king, James, if "To build some statelie house is his intention": "Ah, in this kinde I had too much invention!" (no. 427). Again and again in his writings Harington returns to the subject of building. Technical aspects obviously interested him: in the notes to *Orlando,* he mentions the frail construction of the buildings in Paris, "so high and so sleight": "doubtles," he comments, "it is a great blot in a magnificent citie to see brown paper houses" (16.H). In Harington's version of the poem, it is "the lime new moulten from the wall" that makes the gap through which Iocondo sees the queen at play with her dwarf (28.33).[64] One of the anecdotes in the *Supplie* is about the crowd of tradesmen delivering stone and timber for a great house; another tells of the collapse of an earth and plaster floor in an Irish castle.[65] Harington admired signs of restoration and new building on travels to Gloucester and to Cambridge, and interested himself in church building, not only as a historian in the *Supplie,* but also as an active campaigner for funds.[66]

As well as this practical interest in building, Harington was aware of the role of great houses as outlets for display, symbols of magnificence and extravagance. He asks admiringly in the *Treatise on Playe,* "Who was more magnificent in matters of trew honor, more sumptuows in buildinge, ritch in furnishinge, royall in entertayninge, orderly in maintayninge his howse then Sir Christofer Hatton, late Lord Chawncellor?" The danger in the glittering magnificence of a great house lay not only in its ruinous cost, but also in the overweening ambition it might suggest to those jealous for their own power in the land. In the *Supplie* Harington tells the story of Sir Robert Stapleton, cultured, comely, and rich, who had among his great designs the building of "a faire house or rather Palace," whose "modell . . . he had brought of Italie." When the Arch-bishop of York saw it, he thought its magnificence far beyond what was proper for a mere knight, and the resulting quarrel ruined them both.[67]

For those who had built sumptuously, but (unlike Stapleton) in accordance with their station, the crowning glory was a visit by the queen. In the *Supplie,* Harington describes Bishop Fletcher's triumph when he prevailed on the queen to visit his house, and the special bay window he built for her.[68] Similarly, when the queen visited Kelston in 1592, as part of a royal progress to Oxford, Harington must have felt that his building enterprise had come to a satisfying climax. The fountain at Kelston came into good use on this occasion: according to one account, the queen "dined right royally under the fountain which played in the Court." Poynton says Harington had to sell his estate of St. Katharine's Court to cover the expenses of the queen's visit. In the same year, Harington was High Sheriff of Somerset.[69]

If the story about the origins of the *Orlando* is accurate, Harington must have been banished from the court for some time before the translation was finished in 1591; and it seems that he fell from favor again in 1596 when the *Metamorphosis* was published. In between, he seems to have been often at court, and the series of notes that Henry Harington collected from the Harington papers for the vol-umes of *Nugae Antiquae* include a number of reflections on life at court in this period.[70] One echoes a tradition of comparing the court unfavorably with the pastoral life: at Kelston, Mall, the children and even the animals are "well fedde, well taughte, and well be-lovede"; at court, there is only "ill breeding with ill feedinge, and no love but that of the lustie god of gallantrie." Others suggest dread of the displeasure of the powerful: the story of the queen's savage anger at a courtier's "fringed clothe" provokes the remark, "Heav'n spare me from suche jibinge."

There are gratifying moments, too: Mall's comfits have been praised by the queen; the queen has called for Harington's arm to rest on; the queen has admired his "laste frize jerkin." But when *"The sunne dothe not shine"* at court and there is no point in trying any suit, when envy and jealousy surround the courtier, then there is despair:

Now, what findethe he who lovethe the "pride of life," the cowrtes vanitie, ambition's puff ball? In soothe, no more than emptie wordes, grinninge scoffe, watching nightes, and fawning daies.

"I have spente my time, my fortune, and almoste my honestie," he says in another note, "to buy false hope, false friends, and shallow praise."

Harington's literary activities in the 1590s were mostly satirical. The epigrams, which date mainly from this period, have a good deal to say about court figures as well as about domestic matters like relations with Mall and Lady Rogers. "I will write a damnable storie," Harington says in one of the notes, "and put it in goodlie verse, about Lord A——; he hathe done me some ill turnes." The queen inspired more lyrical poetry—her asking for his arm to support her will be a "swete burden to my nexte songe"; "Petrarcke shall eke out good matter for this businesse."[71] Sir Walter Raleigh, "Paulus," swaggers through the epigrams, along with a gallery of self-important, hypocritical and colorful rogues, male and female. Although the epigrams were not published in Harington's lifetime—he says in one of them that they were not written for sale, but for the pleasure of his friends and himself (no. 424)—they seem to have circulated widely, to judge from contemporary references and from the multiple manuscript versions in which they survive.[72]

With the *Orlando* translation and the circulation of his epigrams in the courtly circle, Harington must have achieved some reputation as a poet by the late 1590s. There is some confirmation of this in the epigram that tells of a writer who published a list of poets and thought he would grieve Harington by leaving him out of it; Harington's retort is that his works are their own praise (no. 202).[73]

The literary scene of the day—to judge from Harington's references to fellow-poets in his writings—was dominated by Sir Philip Sidney. There is no indication that he had met Sidney, who died in 1587, but he had a complete manuscript of *Astrophil and Stella*—he lent it to a neighbor in Kelston on one occasion—and knew the first, unpublished version of *Arcadia*. He cites *Astrophil* and *Arcadia* as authorities for literary practice, and elsewhere refers readers to Sidney's *Apology for Poetry* for questions of literary theory.[74]

Second to Sidney, in Harington's eyes, is probably Edmund Spenser: soon after the first three books of *The Faerie Queene* were published, they were given a favorable notice in Harington's *Orlando*

(43.M); in 1596, in the *Metamorphosis*, he mentions the new edition of the poem and commends its author warmly.[75] Listing the leading poets of the day, Harington includes Samuel Daniel and Henry Constable as well as Sidney and Spenser (epigram no. 196). He and Daniel wrote verses on the same picture for the Earl of Hertford;[76] Constable he calls his "very good friend" in *Orlando* (34.A), and quotes in his *Tract on the Succession*. Another poet he seems to have regarded as a colleague was Sir John Davies, as an epigram indicates (no. 112). Davies has a poem of his own on the picture of Bungey (Harington's spaniel) on the *Orlando* title page, and they seem often to have chosen the same subjects for satire.[77]

Harington's next venture into print after the *Orlando* was *A New Discourse of a Stale Subject, Called the Metamorphosis of Ajax* (1596). It presents a technical innovation in domestic sanitation—an improved privy, complete with a flushing system—embedded in an extraordinary paraphernalia of mock learning, irreverent innuendo, shameless advertisement of the author and his friends, and miscellaneous verse and anecdote on the indecorous subject of Harington's invention. There was also a good deal of satire, directed at individuals (much of it now obscure) and more generally exploiting the privy for moralizing—pointing out the hypocrisy of those who find privies offensive but wink at sin, and suggesting that having sweetened the privy, the more serious task of purifying souls remains to his readers.

In spite of the trappings, Harington, it seems, was serious about his invention. His pamphlet is a contribution to good domestic architecture: he argues that no amount of decorative adornment will make a house habitable if its design does not include well-ventilated privies. If anyone is interested in installing the device, he says, "I will come home to his house to him, I will read him a lecture of it, I will instruct his workmen, I will give him plots and models. . . ."[78] Two letters from 1602 suggest he was doing all these things for the houses of Sir Robert Cecil and the Earl of Shrewsbury.[79] A "perfumed privy" to Harington's design was built at Richmond Palace, according to an epigram (no. 45).

It is also true that Harington exploited the scandalous subject matter of his book for its publicity value. He was, as he says in a letter in 1596, "the willinger to wryte such a toye as this, because, I had layne me thought allmost buryed in the Contry these three or fowre yeere; and I thought this would give some occasion to have me thought of and talked of."[80]

He was certainly talked of, but with amazement rather than admiration: amazement, mainly, that a man of his social standing had written a book on an unsavory topic more fitting for a jester than a courtier.[81] As Grimble points out, Harington had already been rebuked for involving himself in the trade of printing; now in the *Metamorphosis* he was concerning himself with the baser aspects of plumbing.[82] As late as 1599 a cloud of scandal hung over Harington's name at court. The queen was only then beginning to forgive her indiscreet godson. The question of bringing Harington before the Star Chamber had even been raised.[83]

This period of royal disfavor must have meant exile from court. It was probably about this time that Harington wrote his *Treatise on Playe,* on the problem of excessive gambling. Along the way, he offers many insights into life at court. Ideally, the court is "that house whence the pattern and lyght of all honor and order should come." Realistically, Harington admits how boring it is at court for those in attendance for long hours in the presence chamber— "men cannot be allways discowrsing" there, nor women always sewing. He even has something to say on the hardness of the seats, "that, since great breeches were layd asyde, men can skant indewr to sitt on."[84] His solution to the gambling problem takes account of the importance of making a grand show in a place like the court: he suggests play should be for high denominations (in public) but they should then be valued at a fraction of their face value when settling debts (in private).

1599–1603: Service in Ireland and the Succession from Elizabeth to James

The signal for Harington's return to royal favor was a summons to go to Ireland with the new Lord Lieutenant, the Earl of Essex. Charles Blount, Lord Mountjoy, had been intended for the mission of quelling the rebellion in Ireland by Hugh O'Neill, Earl of Tyrone, but Essex defeated Mountjoy's supporters in the Privy Council and took the job for himself. A letter to Harington from his cousin, Robert Markham, warned him that all was not as it seemed with Essex's mission: "Essex hath enemies; he hath friendes too: now there are two or three of Montjoy's kindred sent oute in your armie;

they are to report all your conduct to us at home." The suspicion was that Essex "goeth not forthe to serve the Queenes realme, but to humour his owne revenge."[85]

A letter from Essex to Harington in 1599 informed him that the queen had specially commended him to Essex for the Irish mission; Harington was to have a troop of horsemen under the command of the Earl of Southampton. Harington later said that he hardly had time to put on his boots when he was called to follow Essex.[86] The expedition landed at Dublin on 14 April.[87] Instead of moving north to attack Tyrone in Ulster, as had been planned, Essex set off early in May to secure garrisons and subdue rebellion to the south, in Leinster and Munster. Meanwhile, a detachment of forces had been sent to Connaught, to the west, under Sir Conyers Clifford. Included in this group were Sir Griffin Markham—Harington's cousin—and Harington himself.

They left Dublin on 9 May and spent some six weeks in Connaught. The journey was eventful, with ambushes from the rebels in places like woods and fords, where they were at a disadvantage, but they arrived with few losses. Harington spent most of his time with the garrison at Roscommon and remained in health, though many with him sickened through "drinking water, and milk, and vinegar, and aqua vitae, and eating raw beef at midnight, and lying upon wet green corn oftimes, and lying in boots, with heats and colds."[88]

Essex returned to Dublin from Leinster and Munster at the beginning of July. Later in that month, he set out for a campaign in Leix and Offaly; Sir Conyers Clifford, Sir Griffin Markham, Harington, the Earl of Kildare, and their troops set off from Connaught to meet him at Fercal in Offaly. On the way, the rebels' lands were burned and pillaged by various companies, some on foot, "so that," Harington says, "all the countrey was on fire at once, and our comming was so unlook'd for, that in the towns where we came, the rebels had no leisure to carry their young children, much lesse their corn and other stuff."[89]

On 30 July, when the two armies parted, Essex used his power as viceroy to give Harington and a number of others "the honour of knighthood in the field." Sir Conyers Clifford then set off to relieve Collooney near Sligo; in a pass through the Curlew Mountains, his army was attacked by the forces of O'Donnell and defeated, in a catastrophic reverse for the English. Harington, who was with

Clifford, says that as the enemy numbers increased the English footmen fell back "in rout," dismayed by a lack of munitions or some other unknown cause. Clifford was killed; some honor was saved by the horsemen, who "gave a desperate charge upon the hill, among rocks and bogs, where never horse was seen to charge before; it is verily thought they had all been cut in peices. . . ." Sir Griffin Markham was wounded; Harington escorted him to safety in a horse-litter and took up residence at Trim, a town some thirty miles from Dublin, from where he wrote his account of the battle to his servant, Thomas Combe, on 31 August.[90]

Essex set out from Dublin once again on 28 August, this time in hopes of joining battle with the rebel Tyrone and his army. There was no pitched battle, but Tyrone arranged a meeting with Essex, alone, at Ballaclinth Ford, and a truce was arranged by 8 September. It seems that Essex promised to present Tyrone's terms to the queen in person; he left Ireland for London on 24 September.

Late in October, Harington was still in Ireland waiting for a ship to return him to England. He reports that he has spent his time in traveling with Sir William Warren to meet Tyrone at Dundalk. The earl, whom he had met in England, treated him with respect. Leaving the earl and Sir William to their negotiations, Harington talked to the earl's sons and their tutors and presented them with a copy of his Ariosto; later he read some passages to the earl, "which he seemed to like so well, that he solemnly swore his boys should read all the book over to him." Harington's account of the conversation and its setting borrows the imagery of a pastoral Golden Age, and some biblical phrasing:

Other pleasant and idle tales were needless and impertinent, or to describe his fern table and fern forms, spread under the stately canopy of heaven. His guard, for the most part, were beardless boys without shirts; who, in the frost, wade as familiarly through rivers as water-spaniels. With what charm such a master makes them love him I know not, but if he bid come, they come; if go, they do go; if he say do this, they do it.[91]

He found the Irish much given to whoring and to abusive discourse; but they were welcoming to strangers, and he himself had been happy to enjoy their hospitality. Being sent to fight against one group of Irishmen seemed no reason not to eat with others. He prided himself on his knowledge of the country—gained from observation and discussion—and felt his reception there might be "a presage of a fortune I might rise to in this kingdom."[92]

Harington returned to England in November, arriving at Richmond on the sixth. His reception by the queen, in the midst of the gathering storm over Essex, was not promising: "she frownede and saide, 'What, did the foole brynge *you* too? Go back to your businesse.' " In another letter he says:

I came to court in the very heat and height of all displeasures: after I had been there but an hour, I was threatened with the Fleet; I answered poetically, "that coming so late from the land-service, I hoped that I should not be prest to serve in her Majesty's fleet in Fleet-street [i.e., in the Fleet Prison]."[93]

Essex was accused, principally, of having wasted his opportunity by campaigning in Munster instead of in Ulster when he first arrived in Ireland, and with having left his post without permission to return to England. His creation of numerous knights as viceroy had also given offense, and the fact that he had parleyed with the archrebel Tyrone without witnesses was held to be incriminating.[94]

After some days, the queen gave Harington an audience "in the withdrawing chamber at Whitehall," and, to Harington's great relief, withdrew her worst threats. It was probably on this occasion that he showed her the journal he had kept in Ireland; the queen "swore, 'by God's Son, we were all idle knaves, and the Lord Deputy worse, for wasting our time and hir commandes, in such wyse as my Journale dothe write of.' " His knighthood was a particularly sore point with the queen.[95]

Harington was back in Kelston by December 1599 and spent the winter there, relieved to have escaped the storms of court. He described himself as "a private country knight, that lives among clouted shoes, in his frize jacket and galloshes, and who envies not the great commanders of Ireland."[96]

In 1600 he journeyed to the North of England to establish his claim to the Harington manors by taking possession in person; his legal title was in dispute and there was some resistance. A letter from Sir Robert Sidney informed him that his Irish adventures were less talked of at court, and urged him to please the queen all he could to further his suit for the northern manors. Harington was indeed intending to please Her Majesty, perhaps with a gift of five

hundred pounds and "some prety Jewel or garment." His efforts
came to nothing.[97]

Meanwhile, Essex had been imprisoned and was tried for his
offenses in Ireland in June 1600. Harington continued to see him;
he mentions a contrite message he was to carry from Essex to the
queen, and, after another meeting, noted how "ambition thwarted
in its career, dothe speedilie leade on to madnesse." Essex

shyftethe from sorrowe and repentaunce to rage and rebellion so suddenlie,
as well provethe him devoide of goode reason or righte mynde . . . he
uttered strange wordes borderinge on suche strange desygns, that made
me hasten forthe and leave his presence. Thank heaven! I am safe at home,
and if I go in suche troubles againe, I deserve the gallowes for a meddlynge
foole.[98]

In February 1601 Essex turned to open rebellion. As a modern
historian puts it, "faced with bankruptcy, and in the midst of
unendurable nervous tension, he called upon the London mob for
aid."[99] Harington, it seems, was one of those who protected the
queen during the rebellion. After its suppression, Essex was executed. Harington, who had known Essex since his Cambridge days—
in twenty years, he says, he "omitted no office of a kynde freind
to him"—regretted that the queen had not been more merciful to
the hotheaded earl.[100]

A letter of 1601 shows that Harington spent six weeks at court
that year, but was not welcome there: Lord Buckhurst was told,
"Go tell that witty fellow, my godson, to get home: it is no season
now to foole it here." Harington reported that the queen "walks
much in her privy chamber, and stamps with her feet at ill news,
and thrusts her rusty sword at times into the arras in great rage."[101]

By the end of 1602 the queen was in a "moste pitiable state."
She inquired after Harington's literary efforts, and he read her some
verses "whereat she smilede once, and was pleasede to saie;—'When
thou doste feele creepinge tyme at thye gate, these fooleries will
please thee lesse; I am paste my relishe for such matters.' " She died
on 24 March 1603. Harington determined to rest his troubled mind
in Kelston, "and tende my sheepe like an Arcadian swayne, that
hathe loste his faire mistresse; for in soothe, I have lost the beste
and faireste love that ever shepherde knew, even my gracious Queene."
In a long letter to Robert Markham in 1606, he described her hold

on those around her, her mercurial temperament, penetrating mind, and sharp wit. "When she smiled, it was a pure sun-shine, that every one did chuse to baske in, if they could; but anon came a storm from a sudden gathering of clouds, and the thunder fell in wondrous manner on all alike. I never did fynde greater show of understandinge and lerninge, than she was bleste wyth. . . ."[102]

For all his loyalty to the queen, Harington did not neglect the problem of who was to be her successor, and how he was to gain the newcomer's favor. In 1591 he sent a copy of the *Orlando Furioso* translation to James VI of Scotland. In 1602, he wrote (but did not publish) his *Tract on the Succession to the Crown,* arguing that James was the rightful heir to the English throne and devoting a chapter to fulsome flattery of the Scottish king. Perhaps his most remarkable exercise in "court-craft," as the *Nugae Antiquae* calls it, was a lantern of gold, silver, brass, and iron, sent as a New Year's gift along with a copy of Harington's epigrams to James for Christmas 1602. Its reflector inside was embossed with the sun, moon, and seven stars; on the other side were engraved illustrations of the birth and passion of Christ. Clearly, James was the rising sun in Harington's emblem, and perhaps even a Saviour: one of the Latin mottoes on the lantern was the text "Lord, remember me when thou comest in thie kingdom."[103]

In 1603 Harington celebrated James's triumphal entry at Burleigh as King of England in "A gratulatory Elegy" (epigram no. 425). In private, however, he was scornful of those who eagerly offered themselves in the service of the new king. In a letter of April 1603 he says he is a cripple "not made for sportes in newe cowrtes," and prefers to read Petrarch, Horace, "and such wise ones" in the country.[104]

1603–12: Prison, Star Chamber; Prose and Poetry for King James and Prince Henry

Harington's fortunes took a disastrous turn in May 1603. He had "played the foole to frendly," in his own phrase, and offered surety for a debt of his uncle, Thomas Markham, for four thousand pounds. The credit was used by Markham's son-in-law, Sir John Skinner, to buy an estate at Barwick, in Somerset; Skinner was unable to pay the debt and Harington, as guarantor, was arrested for debt in May and placed in the Gate-House Prison, Westminster. Through

Lord Cecil and Sir Thomas Erskine, Harington appealed to the king for relief, as, in his words, "the Principalls have both means and mynds to sell lands to pay theyr detts"; he owed nothing on his own behalf. [105]

By July further calamity had fallen on the house of Markham, calamity that as it turned out offered Harington a way out of his difficulties. Thomas Markham's son, Sir Griffin Markham, who had been Harington's companion in arms in Ireland in 1599, was implicated in the Bye plot to depose James and put Arabella Stuart on the throne, and arrested. Harington sued the king for the forfeiture of Markham's lands, to pay Thomas Markham's debt. A year later, they were granted him. [106]

From a letter written in October 1603 it appears that Harington had fled from the Gate-House Prison shortly before, by his own account aiming to avoid the plague rather than the debt. His wife had taken up residence in Cannon Row; after the escape, Dobbinson, the Bailiff of Westminster, broke in there and had an altercation with her. In these troubled days Harington apparently relied on his friendship with Cecil, the queen's chief minister. Cecil's patience had its limits, as a draft letter of October in this year shows: incensed that Harington had rebuked him for his "passion," he tells him that such admonishment "was as superfluous as many other labors of yours, which I coud never conn without booke." He pictures Harington as a self-appointed moral arbiter, whose ill-judged and elaborately learned "censorious writings" come from a pen "men say is alwaies so full of inke as in many of your writings many blotts droppe upon the paper." He signs himself "Your loving frend," nevertheless. [107]

Harington was bidden to a private audience with the king, probably late in 1603. [108] James declared that he had heard much of Harington's learning and wit, questioned him about philosophy, Satan, and witches, and asked to be read a passage from the *Orlando*. He quoted from philosophers Harington had never read, and warned him not to read certain others which would lead him to "evile consultations." Harington's answers, by his own report, included "a scurvey jeste" on witches and a quip about the physical evils Satan had inflicted on his body; he was careful to be modest about his attainments, "as not willinge a subjecte shoulde be wiser than his Prince, nor even appeare so." [109]

The acquisition of Sir Griffin Markham's estates and the sale of land at Lenton in Nottinghamshire enabled Harington to clear himself of the Markham debt. By 20 May 1604 he could report the matter "allmost overblowne"; by then, however, a new crisis had arisen. This time it came from his wife's family. His brother-in-law Edward Rogers brought an action against him in the Star Chamber. Rogers alleged that Harington, while his mother-in-law was on her deathbed in Bath in 1602, took the keys to her house at Cannington, and "in ryotouse manner ryfled the said Howse," carrying off five thousand pounds in plate and cash belonging to Edward Rogers and his son Francis; and after Lady Rogers's death, returned to the house and "burned and razed the Evidences of the said Edward Rogers." Harington states as defendant that his first visit was at Lady Rogers's wish, and that there was no more than twenty pounds' worth of plate and cash at the house; his second visit, he claims, was on behalf of his wife as executor, and none of Rogers's "evidence" was burned at the time. By 17 June 1604 the case had been dealt with and referred to the arbitration of three lords and two judges; Harington felt that the case had had "a very honorable and full heeringe." By July he regarded his troubles as over, and himself as restored to the king's favor. [110]

James's heir was Prince Henry Frederick, though in the event the prince died before his father. In 1604 Harington sent James a translation of *Aeneid*, Book 6, with a commentary, for Henry's use. He says he has returned to his translation—completed earlier for his own son—encouraged by his reading in his time of "to[o] long leysure," by which he perhaps means his imprisonment in 1603. He has added the commentary for the further edification of the prince and has amended some scansion in the translation, correcting mistakes first brought to his notice by "the tendernes of yo*u*r Majesties ear," possibly at the interview of 1603. [111]

This was followed in June 1605 by the presentation of a volume of Harington's epigrams to the prince; Harington hastens to associate them with his youth rather than his present state of "gray hairs" and "grave thoughts." He was evidently anxious in these years to present himself as a reformed character. A letter of 1602 regrets that his poetry has hindered him from better studies. [112] "The authors farewell to his Muse," of April 1603, is the most extended treatment of this theme: the new age and the new king will require of him "a Muse awsteare," and he offers a devoted service that will allow no leisure for "wanton toyes" (no. 427). In the epistle to the king prefixed to the *Aeneid* translation he refers to this poem, and hopes specifically that his former spending ("or rather mispending") of so much time upon trifles will "be no preiudyce to any future employment that my breeding hath made mee otherwyse capable of." It was in this chastened mood that he applied for the Archbishopric of Dublin and the Lord Chancellorship of Ireland; as we have seen, his pleas were to no avail, and he made no third journey to Ireland.

He continued to appear at court, as the famous letter of 1606 on the masque at Theobalds in honor of the Danish king indicates. His account is a satiric one: much the worse for drink, the queen of Sheba approached King James and his royal guest bearing precious gifts, but tripped and tipped her offerings of food and drink into the Danish king's lap; Hope and Faith could not bring out their lines, and were sick in the lower hall; Peace, at her entry, "most rudely made war with her olive branch, and laid on the pates of those who did oppose her coming." Harington wished himself at home in the country.[113]

His attentions to Prince Henry were more enthusiastic. In 1608 he presented the prince with his *A Supplie or Addicion to the Catalogue of Bishops,* written in late 1607 and early 1608. It is a set of lives of the bishops of the Church of England, and generally supports them against Puritan dissenters, while condemning those who created fortunes for themselves and their families out of Church property after the Reformation.

In July 1607 Harington was present when King James and Prince Henry dined at the Merchant Taylors' Hall and were entertained with lutes, organs, and singing. Among the projects Harington pursued in this year were attempts to persuade Thomas Sutton to make the king's son Charles, Duke of York, his heir, in exchange for a barony (much to Sutton's alarm), and to have Sutton and others contribute to the repair of Bath Abbey. Harington and Sutton were both involved in land dealings connected with the Markham affair and apparently had a shared enemy in Sir John Skinner.[114]

In the same year, Harington entered a controversy with Bishop Hall over the marriage of clergy and published his translation of the *Regimen Sanitatis Salernitanum,* a medieval handbook of health from which he had already quoted in the *Metamorphosis.* It was the third of his works to be published, after the *Orlando* in 1591 and the *Metamorphosis* in 1596, and the last to be published in his lifetime.

A letter to Harington from Lord Thomas Howard at about this time illuminates Harington's assets and liabilities as a courtier to King James. Howard says the king has asked after him, calling him "the 'merry blade.' " James is eager for learned discourse, which Harington can supply, but as well as such "endowments of the inward sort," one must remember the "special affection" of men like the king "towards outward thinges, cloaths, deportment, and good countenance." Harington is no longer young or handsome, Howard says: his attainments in Latin, Greek, Italian, and Spanish are not really sought after at court; more in request is outrageous flattery of Carr, the royal favorite, or of the king's roan horse.[115]

Instead of praising the king's horse, Harington directed his efforts to the Prince of Wales, sending him the *Supplie* and letters about his own dog Bungey. Bungey had been celebrated in a epigram (no. 219) and in the *Orlando* volume; on this occasion, in 1608, his feats as messenger and carrier, his kidnap and captivity by the Spanish ambassadors, and his manner of dying are celebrated.[116]

In 1609 Harington is again writing for the prince's amusement, incorporating some family history and some royal verses from his collection in his letter, and sending a copy of his *Orlando*. He continued his interest in the repair of Bath Abbey; notes in his papers suggest he was occupied with housekeeping and matters of plumbing and draining on his Kelston estate: a "pump and forse for the pryvyes" is mentioned, and a system of ponds, fountains, and vaults described.[117]

As early as the 1590s, Harington had commended the singing of Psalms; notwithstanding a suggestion in the *Supplie* that poetry and divinity are better kept separate, he turned in the last years of his life to his own metrical paraphrase of the Psalms. Letters from 1612 show that in spite of sickness in that year, Harington was anxious to promote his translations, and to have them published. His confidence in his own powers was undiminished: in a letter to King James asking for his support for the project, he declared his opinion that few divines could have achieved such holy poetry, and fewer poets could have delivered divinity in verse so faithfully.[118]

Harington is reported "sicke of a dead palsie" in May 1612. He died in November that year—two weeks before Prince Henry—

and was buried at Kelston in December. His wife, Mary, lived until
1634. Seven of Harington's children survived him, including his
eldest son, John, who achieved fame as a Puritan Parliamentarian
and diarist.[119]

Chapter Two

Orlando Furioso and *Aeneid,* Book 6: Harington's Translation and Commentary

Ariosto's *Orlando*

Ariosto's *Orlando Furioso,* first published in Ferrara in 1516, was well known in England by Harington's time. Stanzas were frequently included in miscellanies and collections, and longer extracts had appeared in translation or paraphrase.[1] Thomas Byrd wrote an early madrigal based on some of Ariosto's verses;[2] one of the stanzas he chose may serve as an introduction to the poem (the prose translations that follow Ariosto's lines here and below are by Allan Gilbert):

> La verginella è simile alla rosa,
> ch'in bel giardin su la nativa spina
> mentre sola e sicura si riposa,
> né gregge né pastor se le avicina;
> l'aura soave e l'alba rugiadosa,
> l'acqua, la terra al suo favor s'inchina:
> gioveni vaghi e donne inamorate
> amano averne e seni e tempie ornate.

(The young virgin is like the rose that neither flock nor shepherd draws near to while it rests alone and secure in a beautiful garden on its native thorn. The soft breeze and the dewy dawn, the water, the earth bend to favor her; gracious youths and enamoured women love to have their breasts and foreheads decked with her.) (1.42)[3]

This is a limpid and lyrical variation on the theme of virginity; its context makes it a less straightforward affair than it first appears, however. It is spoken by the Saracen warrior Sacripante, and he is thinking of his lost mistress, the beautiful Angelica, who he fears may already have sacrificed her virginity. But Angelica is in fact

close by, hiding in a grove of the forest, and emerges on hearing
Sacripante's lament, not to offer him solace but to make use of his
protection. Sacripante responds by resolving to pluck the morning
rose of her virginity himself, but he is thwarted by the untimely
arrival of another knight, whom he duly challenges to battle. In
this way the mingling of matters of love and feats of arms, and the
chance encounters of the forest and the waywardness of human
impulses, generate one incident after another in the poem, in a
richly abundant and varied stream of narrative. Equally, it is clear
that the conventions of romance are manipulated in a special way
in Ariosto's narrative: here and elsewhere, a play of ironies brings
his characters, episodes, and above all his chivalric materials into
sharp focus. Ariosto is heir to the accumulated traditions of Arthur
and Charlemagne and their knights, but he also looks forward to
the complexities of *Don Quixote,* pitting human nature against chivalric ideals and common sense against the marvels of romance.

The setting for *Orlando Furioso* is the invasion of France by the
Moors and the struggle of Christian Europe, led by Charlemagne,
to resist it. In the war of the two armies the siege of Paris is the
centerpiece, but combats between individual knights away from the
battlefield are just as important; and more important still to Ariosto's design are matters of love, which are the mainsprings of the
two principal plots. The title of the poem comes from Orlando's
hopeless infatuation for Angelica, which drives him mad ("furioso")
when she gives herself to another; the long courtship of the Saracen
champion Ruggiero and the Christian warrior-maiden Bradamante
forms the other main plot.

The love between Ruggerio and Bradamante is heroic love, sanc-
tioned by Providence as the foundation of the house of Este, the
rulers of Ferrara, who were Ariosto's patrons. Here the two principles
of love and epic struggle are in harmony; elsewhere in the poem,
however, love and arms are more like opposites. Love is most often
undignified and destructive; it distracts knights from battle, defies
the rules of chivalry when it turns to lust, and frequently upsets
decorum by settling on an unworthy object.

Among all the conventions Ariosto inherited, it is the marvels
of romance that prompt his subtlest irony. His attitude is poised
between mockery of their childish improbability and nostalgia for
the world they conjure up. One such marvel is the castle of the
magician Atlante. He creates it by his sorcery to keep his nephew

Ruggiero protected from the perils of the world of knightly struggle. Atlante captures selected knights and ladies to keep Ruggiero company in luxurious imprisonment in the castle; by his art, he makes himself appear to be the object of each knight's and lady's desire in turn. In this way, he keeps his captives bound by the strength of their own longing, condemned to a fruitless and perpetual search through the halls and chambers of his palace (13.50). Bradamante, in spite of warnings, is drawn into the castle by one of Atlante's illusions, a fleeting, deceiving vision of her beloved Ruggiero (13.75–79). Finally the enchantment is broken by Astolfo, with the help of his horn and a book of remedies, which has the antidote for the spell of the castle conveniently listed in its index (22.16–23). The traditional material of enchantments, frustrated love, and knightly questing becomes charged, as the narrative unfolds, with a supremely intelligent, provocative commentary on human motives and dilemmas: without ever being able quite to define any straightforward allegory or moral, the reader begins to see that though Ariosto's marvels are a delightful liberation from the physical laws of cause and effect, in human terms they serve only as a clearer index to the delusions of love and the perplexities of fate.

There are examples of explicit allegories in the poem, too: the magic ring, which is called the ring of reason; the rock of Logistilla, which clearly represents the moral life in contrast to Alcina's island, where sensual indulgence reigns; and the characters who are named Silence, Hypocrisy, and Discord. Such transparent moralizing is never allowed to dominate in the poem, however. Most of all, Ariosto's work is dedicated to the pleasures of narrative, with different strands interlaced as he says like the threads of a tapestry, the chords of a song, the courses of a banquet, or the paths of a forest, so that the reader is challenged to keep track of proliferating interrupted stories, a game that comes to stretch his powers of memory to and beyond their limit.

There are also moments of action and feeling in the poem that escape the modifying forces of narrative irony from within and authorial irony from without. In canto 16, for instance, the terrible progress of the pagan king Rodomonte through the Christian defenders of Paris—he leaves a wide swath of fire and destruction, and mountains of dead—closes the reader for once within a narrative world free of irony, until the poet switches abruptly to a separate narrative strand in the next canto. In canto 29, to quote one last episode from the poem, the gentle Isabella falls into Rodomonte's power; the bloodthirsty Saracen is intent on raping her. She buys time by pretending she has the secret of a magic ointment that makes its wearer invulnerable; she prepares it, puts it on her neck, and invites Rodomonte to try its power by using his sword on her. Duped by the trick, he sweeps off her head. By this desperate stratagem she saves her honor at the cost of her life. The moving elegy on Isabella that follows (29.26–29) has already been quoted in Harington's translation. Harington chose to apply it to his own mother, Isabell, just as Ariosto no doubt had Isabella d'Este, from the family of his patron, and perhaps other Isabellas of the time, in mind.

This, then, was the splendidly varied, colorful, and sparklingly intelligent poem Englishmen were reading and translating in the 1580s and 1590s; most importantly, of course, it was then providing the inspiration for *The Faerie Queene,* of which the first part appeared in 1590, the year before Harington's *Orlando.*

Harington's *Orlando*

Perhaps the clearest way of conveying how Harington made an English poem out of Ariosto's text is to follow the fortunes of one canto of *Orlando Furioso* in his translation. For this purpose canto 10 seems appropriate: it contains material from various narrative strands: the story of Olimpia and Bireno, the adventures of Ruggiero with Alcina and Logistilla, and Ruggiero's encounter with the most desirable beauty of the *Orlando,* Angelica. It presents Ariosto at his most varied, giving the reader in a short span moralizing, pathos, adventure, irony, epic display, suspense, and eroticism.

The canto begins by moralizing the fate of Olimpia, most faithful of lovers, who is now about to be deserted by her new husband, Bireno. Here Harington translates stanza for stanza. A characteristic touch is to change Ariosto's light reminder that the carelessness of lovers like Bireno ignores God's omniscience—they carry on "senza guardar che Dio tutto ode e vede" ("without considering that God hears and sees everything," 10.5)—into a firm final couplet on the inevitability of the divine vengeance: such lovers neglect the fact "That God doth see and know their falsehood still / And can and shall revenge it at his will" (10.5).

With the next section of the Canto, the account of Bireno's desertion of Olimpia (10.10–34), Harington begins to omit substantial portions of the original. He leaves out many of the narrative details Ariosto uses to intensify the pathos of the situation—the cry of the halcyon birds lamenting "l'antico infortunio" ("their ancient misfortune," 10.20), the fact that the rock Olimpia climbs to seek Bireno is hollowed out by the waves and bends out over the ocean, making a telling image of her feelings (10.23)—and adds general sentiments of his own: "Her wofull words might move the stones and stocks" (10.23), "thus with wicked practise and unjust / He her forsooke that chiefly him did trust" (10.19). A mournful repetition in the original, however ("Bireno chiama; e al nome di Bireno / rispondean gli Antri che pietà n'avieno" ["She shouts: 'Bireno,' and with the name of Bireno the caverns that pitied her answered," 10.22]), is matched by one in the translation: "Then once or twise she cald *Byrenos* name; / Then once or twise the caves resound the same" (10.22).

The third section of the canto turns abruptly to deal with Ruggiero's escape from Alcina's last attempts to capture him and her defeat by her sister Logistilla. Here Harington has fifteen stanzas to Ariosto's twenty-two, and the omissions are striking. Where Ariosto devotes three stanzas to the details of Ruggiero's discomfort in the blinding heat, the boiling sand, his nearly red-hot armor, his thirst and fatigue, his lips sculpted by thirst and his face covered in sweat (10.35, 36, 38), Harington says simply that Ruggiero ". . . traveld in the hot and sandie way, / Full many werie and unpleasant mile" (10.33).

Just as striking as this pruning of description is Harington's compression of parts of the narrative. In the battle with Alcina's navy, for instance, where in the original the boatman tells Ruggiero to use his magic blinding shield on the enemy, and himself pulls off the cover to dazzle the sailors on the approaching ships (10.49–50), Ruggiero in Harington's version relies solely on Logistilla's artillery to keep Alcina's navy at bay (10.42–43).

The smaller omissions in Harington's version are perhaps even more telling. One category may suffice to illustrate: Ariosto's sound effects. The halcyons whose lament is heard in the original, but nowhere in Harington, have already been mentioned; the turbulence created by Alcina's galleys echoes from sea to shore in Ariosto (10.49), but not in Harington; we hear nothing there, either, of the trumpet blast that brings Alcina's navy to battle in Ariosto's stanza 53. Harington adds a convincing curse to those Alcina's enraged damsels

shower on Ruggiero (the second half of this couplet is Harington's
own): "But burned maist thon be, or cut in quarters / Or driven
to hang thy selfe in thine own garters" (10.37). Harington's characteristically proverbial expression gives us "*Alcyna* wrathfull striv-
ing tooth and naile" (10.42).

The next section of the canto describes Ruggiero's stay on Logistilla's island. Here the transformations wrought by Harington's
translation are intriguing. For instance, Ariosto often remarks on
the world he is describing in such a way as to draw attention to his
hyperbole, to distance himself by a suggestion of irony from the
perfection of this imagined world. In 10.58 he airily suggests that
anyone who wishes to get an idea of the richness of Logistilla's palace
must go there himself, since there is nowhere else like it, except
perhaps in heaven; 10.63 dilates on Logistilla's abilities as a gar-
dener, making perpetual spring without nature's help, "quel che
agli altri impossibile parea" ("something that to others seemed impossible"). In Harington's version, the innuendo disappears. Of
Logistilla's castle "The valew of the walls can no man know / Except
he first upon the same had mounted" (10.49). Logistilla works not
merely without Nature's help, as in Ariosto, but with fountains
watering the plants instead of rain (10.52). James J. Yoch, discussing this and other palaces in *Orlando Furioso,* says rightly, "Harington takes places and characters seriously. Giving less opportunity
for humorous ambiguities or hyperboles, he glosses them as allegories of virtue or vice, and he attempts to locate and place them
in the world."[4]

The descriptions of Logistilla's garden are worth quoting at length
to show the workings of this process (Harington compresses three
of Ariosto's stanzas into two, so that the stanzas below only roughly
correspond).

> Di così nobili arbori non suole
> prodursi fuor di questi bei giardini,
> né di tai rose o di simil viole,
> di gigli, di amaranti o di gesmini.
> Altrove appar come a un medesmo sole
> e nasca e viva, e morto il capo inchini,
> e come lasci vedovo il suo stelo
> il fior suggetto al variar del cielo . . .

(Such noble trees do not grow outside these fair gardens, nor such roses, nor violets like these, nor lilies, nor amaranths, nor jasmines. Elsewhere it seems that under one and the same sun the flower is born and lives and bends its head in death, and that subject to the varying of the heavens it leaves its stalk widowed. . . .) (10.62)

> No weeds or frutelesse trees are in this place
> But herbs whose vertues are of highest price,
> As soveraigne sage and thrift and herbe of grace
> And time, which well bestowed maketh wise,
> And lowly patience, proud thoughts to abase,
> And harts ease that can never grow with vice:
> These are the herbs that in this garden grew,
> Whose vertues do their beauties still renew.
>
> (10.53)

Where Ariosto creates his garden as an opposite to the real world, consciously fantastic, Harington's is transparently allegorical, with the puns on the herb and flower names[5] keeping only a ghostly suggestion of real herbs and flowers in this garden of virtues. Ariosto's playfully regretful suggestions of the impossibility of such a place disappear in Harington's version, and ambiguities collapse into earnestness. Harington's puns give a moral dimension to his garden that threatens to make it fade altogether as an imaginable place.

Ruggiero, having rested a day or two in Logistilla's fair palace and miraculous gardens, makes ready to leave the island on the hippogriff, a magic winged horse. His journey falls into two parts, the first containing his passage to England and the parade of knights and soldiers he saw there, and the second describing his encounter with Angelica and his battle with the orc-monster. The first part comprises stanzas 10.69–90 in the original; for these twenty-two stanzas Harington has nineteen. The omissions come in the geographical details of Ruggiero's journey (10.70 and 71 are reduced to Harington's 10.59) and in the general description of the troops and knights as they gather near the Thames (10.73–76 is rendered in Harington's 10.61–62). One of the details lost here is the sound of the trumpets and drums to which the army assembles in the original (10.74).

In the translation of the catalog of noble leaders and massed troops itself, Harington interpolates descriptions of the dress and temper

of the Scottish and Irish troops (10.73, 74). He adds general observations of his own on travel ("hope of praise makes men no travell
shunne / To say another day: we this have donne," 10.58).

The last section of the canto describes the continuation of Ruggiero's journey. Ariosto's twenty-five stanzas (10.91–115) are com-
pressed into twenty-one of Harington's (10.77–97). For the first
fifteen of them, Harington follows Ariosto stanza for stanza; it is
in the very last part of the canto, the conclusion of the battle with
the sea-monster and Ruggiero's escape with Angelica, that his abridg-
ment takes place. In this part of the canto Ariosto offers some
highlights in description and simile. The picture of Angelica, bound
to the rock, is a variation on the traditional theme of life imitating
art, and the reader shares the shock to Ruggiero's senses as he takes
in the sight:

> Creduto avria che fosse statua finta
> o d'alabastro o d'altri marmi illustri
> Ruggiero, e su lo scoglio così avinta
> per artificio di scultori industri;
> se non vedea la lacrima distinta
> tra fresche rose e candidi ligustri
> fra rugiadose le crudette pome,
> e l'aura sventolar l'aurate chiome.

(Ruggiero would have thought she was a statue, made of alabaster or other
shining marble, and fastened in that way on the rock by the skill of
ingenious sculptors, if he had not seen, among fresh roses and white lilies,
unmistakable tears making the unripe apples dewy, and the breeze stirring
her golden locks.) (10.96)

In Harington's version, the moment of recognition is less pointed,
and the expression more conventional; the rhyme of master/plaster
gives the stanza an epigrammatic cleverness, and the final couplet
generalizes and sentimentalizes Ariosto's description.

> *Rogero* at the first had surely thought
> She was some image made of allablaster
> Or of white marble curiously wrought
> To shew the skilfull hand of some great master,
> But viewing nearer he was quickly taught
> She had some parts that were not made of plaster,

> Both that her eyes did shed such wofull tears
> And that the wind did wave her golden hears.
>
>   (10.82)

There are two stanza-similes in the original (10.103, 105), comparing Ruggiero on the hippogriff attacking the orc to an eagle clawing a snake, and to a fly stinging a dog. In both, the glitter of light and movement and the sudden sound effects in the Italian became plain, direct description in the English; a vivid scene becomes a proverbial comparison.

Harington deals quite summarily with the closing stanzas of the canto. Stanza 106—describing the approach of the monster, beating the water with its tail, and Ruggiero's fears that the hippogriff's wings will become waterlogged and useless—is omitted, with other narrative details.

Ariosto breaks off the canto with provocative suddenness, as Ruggiero is struggling to remove his armor and take advantage of the beautiful Angelica. The situation lends itself to sexual innuendo: Ruggiero makes his steed fold its wings, but does not restrain another charger, which has by now spread *its* wings; he dismounts, but can hardly hold himself back from climbing on a different mount (10.114). Only one of these remarks survives in Harington's hurried version. Ruggiero alights from the hippogriff "But sure it seemd he made his full account / Er long upon a better beast to mount" (10.96).

In general, then, it is fair to say as B. E. Burton does in her thesis that Harington's translation is a "blunting" of the original: the transformation of Ariosto's verse is a process of selection and simplification.[6] The airiness, the glancing ironies, the illusionistic details of Ariosto's romance are brought within a more restricted compass, rendered as a more workaday reality.

Putting Harington's version side by side with his great original inevitably brings out his shortcomings. In fairness, it should also be considered as a poem on its own. Some of Harington's *Orlando,* in any case, is independent of Ariosto. In two cases, he added substantial passages of his own composition to the Italian. In canto 7, Ruggiero is enticed by the witch Alcina into a life lived entirely for pleasure. Harington describes his seduction with gusto: Ruggiero's impatience while he waits between perfumed sheets for Alcina to visit his bed is a fine example:

> Sometime from bed he softly doth arise
> And looke abroad if he might her espie.
> Sometime he with himselfe doth thus devise:
> Now she is comming, now she drawes thus nie.
> Sometime for verie anger out he cries:
> What meaneth she, she doth no faster hie?
>
>   (7.23; cf. Ariosto, 7.25)

To balance this, one of Harington's additions is a homily on the "poysond hooke" of the vain pleasures of the world, which comes shortly after (7.35–37). It begs readers to turn from sin to sober thoughts of God's final reckoning: when that day comes,

> Then shall the vertuous man shine like the sunne,
> Then shall the vicious man repent his pleasure;
> Then one good deed of almes sincerely done
> Shall be more worth then mines of Indian treasure.
> Then sentence shalbe giv'n which none shal shun;
> Then God shal way and pay our deeds by measure.
> Unfortunate and thrise accursed thay
> Whom fond delights do make forget that day . . .
>
>   (7.37)

In Book 15, the English Duke Astolfo travels through the Holy Land with his brothers Grifone and Aquilante. In his 15.73–77, Harington amplifies passing references in Ariosto to the knights' tour of Jerusalem into a full-blown pilgrimage to Jesus' tomb and has each traveler reproach himself in "true remorse devoid of superstition":

> Why then where thou, deare Lord, didst for our sake
> With water and with blood the ground distaine,
> Shall not mine eyes, some small amends to make,
> Shed teares in memorie of so great paine?
> Oh drowsie heart that dost not now awake,
> Oh frosen heart that meltest not in raine,
> Oh stony heart that dost not now relent,
> Lament thee now, or else for ay lament.
>
>   (15.75)

Two qualities especially emerge when Harington's *Orlando* as a whole is looked at as an independent poem: a certain narrative

briskness and a sustained and distinctive voice of resigned worldliness. The quality of impulsion in Harington's stanzas is the compensation for the compression of so many of Ariosto's episodes and
effects, for the flattening of the exquisitely varied contours of the
original *Orlando*. A nineteenth-century translator of the poem, William Stewart Rose, thought Harington's narrative "light and lively
. . . the reader always feels as if he is swimming with the stream."[7]

At its best, the tone of Harington's verse suggests a tolerant,
slightly jaded realism, to match Ariosto's serenely disillusioned irony.
For this voice the *ottava rima* stanza becomes the ideal instrument:
the downbeat of the second line of the final couplet can result in
mere bathos and can interrupt the flow unnecessarily, but it can
also contribute to the sense of cumulation important to epic, em-
phasizing by a slightly weary weightiness the sheer expanse of
narrative.

Sometimes the worldliness is the goodhumored urbanity of By-
ron's *Don Juan*. In Book 25, Ricciardetto tells the story of Fiordispina, who has fallen in love with his sister Bradamante's knightly
exterior, and despairs at finding she is in fact a woman. Sharing a
bed with Bradamante, Fiordispina dreams fitfully of divine assistance: "She thought the gods and heav'n would so assist her / Into
a better sex to chaung my sister" (25.36; cf. Ariosto, 25.44). The
best sustained example of a more resigned, worldly voice occurs in
the stanzas on the region of lost things on the moon, to which
Astolfo travels in Book 34. Ariosto's conception of a vast lumber-
room storing all those things gained or expended in vain on earth
inspires some of Harington's most convincing lines:

> The precious time that fools mispend in play,
> The vaine attempts that never take effect,
> The vows that sinners make and never pay,
> The counsells wise that carelesse men neglect,
> The fond desires that lead us oft astray,
> The prayses that with pride the heart infect,
> And all we loose with follie and mispending
> May there be found unto this place ascending.
>   (34.74: cf. Ariosto, 34.75)

For Ariosto's sophisticated, disillusioned irony, Harington offers
a tolerant realism and a sprightly colloquialism; for his intricate
and labyrinthine narrative, a briskly efficient forward movement;

for his scenes exquisitely detailed in sights and sounds, pictures as plain as a woodcut; for his delicate palaces of fantasy, transparent allegories; and for his ironic finger-wagging, an unabashed sententiousness.

In its own time, the translation won Harington favorable notice, as we have seen.[8] Although Ben Jonson thought it "under all translations was the worst," there were contrary opinions from more temperate critics like Francis Beaumont, who thought that Ariosto "instructed by M. *Harrington* doeth now speake as good English as he did Italian before."[9] Certainly, Harington's translation was widely used. When a translation of passages from Ariosto was called for, Harington's version was borrowed, with or without acknowledgment. Commentators and philosophers like Robert Burton and Francis Bacon drew on the English *Orlando*.[10] It has been suggested that Harington's verse "anticipates, in places, the cadences of Shakespeare's twin poems," *Venus and Adonis* and *The Rape of Lucrece;*[11] Ariosto's story of Adriodante and Genevra is used for the Hero-Claudio plot in *Much Ado About Nothing*—quite possibly by way of Harington's translation—and there is an echo of Harington's verse in *Troilus and Cressida.*[12]

Harington's *Orlando* remained the only complete version of the poem in English until the publication of the translation ascribed to William Huggins, in 1755. There was a second eighteenth-century translation of the whole poem, in heroic couplets, followed by William Stewart Rose's in the nineteenth century, which was not replaced until a series of prose versions and a verse translation in our own century.[13]

Putting Harington's *Orlando* beside the various eighteenth- and nineteenth-century versions, as Lucetta J. Teagarden does in her article on "Theory and Practice in English Versions of *Orlando Furioso*," makes it clear that the passage of time has largely reduced the more recent versions to curiosities, while Harington's still repays reading for its own sake. Partly this is the accident of his having written when he did, and thus having the special claim of being a sixteenth-century translator of a sixteenth-century work; but partly, also, it is a reflection of his spirited response to the original, and his uninhibited transformations of it into an Elizabethan poem. In the examples Teagarden sets out, Harington's translations show a liveliness that compensates for whatever accuracy and clarity his more cautious successors may have achieved.[14] The translations of our own day, of course, serve a different purpose; it is to them we must turn if we want to know what Ariosto said in a particular stanza, or to read the poem through as a modern entertainment. Harington's *Orlando* has some claims, all the same: as a Renaissance translation of a Renaissance poem, and as a considerable achievement in Elizabethan verse.

The Illustrations and Arrangement of Harington's Book

For his translation, Harington used the 1584 edition of *Orlando Furioso,* published in Venice by Francesco de Franceschi. This elaborate volume had an engraved title page, full-page illustrations to each canto, and a critical apparatus including two brief biographies of Ariosto, an exposition of the allegory of the poem, annotations through the text, and a collection of observations on Ariosto's imitations of other authors. It has been called the most sumptuous edition of the poem ever. [15] Harington's book emulates these pictorial and editorial splendors. He includes a substantial preface, defending poetry in general and Ariosto and his own book in particular; marginal annotations and extended notes at the end of each canto; an account of Ariosto's allegory, a biography, an index to the main characters and events of the poem; and a list of "The Principal Tales in Orlando Furioso that may be Read by Themselves" at the end of the book. This profusion of apparatus around the text is an exuberant exploitation of the possibilities of the printed book: using the resources of the printing house to give the reader all possible help in approaching and appreciating Ariosto's poem in its English guise.

Where possible, the engravings in the original by Girolamo Porro have been closely followed in Harington's book. Naturally, something is lost in the process. The chiaroscuro effect of Porro's plates is reduced; figures, especially the smaller ones, are stiffer and relate more awkwardly to their surroundings. The calligraphic fineness of the original and many details of faces and figures are lost. Nevertheless, English readers got some of the essential qualities of the Porro illustrations. Diverse scenes from each canto are arranged in a single design by placing them as if in a landscape stretching from the large, detailed foreground scenes to tiny figures in the background placed in what is almost a map. The English plates, like their originals, give an impression of rich, varied animation, and much of Porro's profusion of detail of costume, armor, caparison, animals, and architecture is kept, as well as his sense of harmonious overall design.

Where it was necessary to make alterations to the originals, Harington and his engravers show their ingenuity. The frontispiece in the Franceschi edition is neatly converted to Harington's purposes. A fine oval head-and-shoulder portrait of the translator (reproduced as the frontispiece of this book) is added, resting against the plinth at the bottom; to the right sits the dog Bungey, looking toward his master's portrait. Harington's frontispiece may well be the first in England to include the portrait of a living writer; it seems to have established a pattern for English translations. Several subsequent ones follow the same plan of showing a portrait of the author above and one of the translator below. [16]

Another adaptation was made necessary by the fact that in Franceschi's edition the illustration for canto 33 was repeated in canto 34. The plate for Book 34 in Harington's edition is skillfully made up from the small woodcut illustration in another Ariosto edition, published by Valgrisi. [17]

Most of the changes in the other illustrations can be attributed to the license allowed the engraver. In two cases, however, there are modifications that may well have been made on Harington's instruction (he says he himself "gave direction" for the making of the plates [17]). Porro did not illustrate any of the inset tales in *Orlando;* [18] in Harington's edition, scenes from these tales are added in the plates for Book 5 and Book 28. In Book 5 it is the story of Ariodante and Genevra—famous as the basis for the Hero-Claudio plot in *Much Ado About Nothing*—which is added, giving special prominence to the balcony scene in which Genevra's maid dressed as her mistress deceives Ariodante into thinking Genevra is being unfaithful to him. In Book 28 the scenes added are from the bawdy story of Iocondo and his search with King Astolfo for an honest woman—the story that is supposed to have led to Harington's translating the whole *Orlando.* Three sexual encounters from the tale are illustrated.

There is a manuscript in the Bodleian Library in Oxford that shows signs of a still more ambitious scheme for an illustrated *Orlando.* [19] It is an early version of the first twenty-four books of Harington's translation, partly in his hand. Each book has at least one plate, mostly from one of the Giolito editions of the 1540s, though two are from Harington's edition as printed (perhaps proofs) and another is an engraving of Andromeda and Perseus, adapted to illustrate Ruggiero's rescue of Angelica from the orc in Book 10. A number of the plates are colored in, some more carefully than others. It seems, then, that Harington drew on at least three different Italian editions of *Orlando* (remembering the Valgrisi woodcut used for Book 34 as well as the Giolito and Franceschi plates) in planning his own edition. He himself declared in his book that the results were as good as any he had seen in England (17). His *Orlando* has been called "the most ambitious book illustrated with metal plates published in the century."[20] The achievement of the illustrations may be compared to the translation itself: much is lost in terms of subtlety and variety; yet a bold outline of the original is conveyed, certain narrative aspects are robustly underlined, and the whole bears the stamp of Harington's irrepressibly individual artistic personality.

"A Briefe Apologie of Poetrie"

Between his dedication to Queen Elizabeth and the first book of his Ariosto Harington inserted a preface, subtitled "A Briefe Apologie of Poetrie and of the Author and Translator of this Poem." The preface is made necessary by those who attack poetry, Harington says: he will deal with objections from those who disapprove of poetry in general, those who object to *Orlando Furioso* in particular, and those whose objection is to Harington's translation and annotation of it. The three different answers make for an unusual combination of discussion in principle about poetry and detailed criticism of a text. Harington makes it clear early on that he regards his preface as the view of an honest practitioner of letters rather than as abstract theory, and declares that he does not intend to discuss "curious definitions" or "subtill distinctions." For such matters the reader is referred to Puttenham's *The Arte of English Poesie,* cited—though its author is not named[21]—with some ironic comments, and to Sidney's *Apology for Poetry.*

Broadly speaking, Harington's defense of poetry is moral and allegorical. There are "many good lessons to be learned" in poetry, "many good examples to be found in it, many good uses to be had of it"; its proper use is to make men capable "of vertue and good discipline" (2). Poets' writings (in particular, those of the "ancient

Poets") contain "divers and sundry meanings": a literal one, a moral one, and deeper still, often a truth from natural philosophy and even from divinity (5). In good poetry "a good and honest and wholesome Allegorie is hidden in a pleasaunt and pretie fiction" (7).

Harington obviously had Sidney's *Apology* very much in mind in composing his own. From incidental proverbial sayings like "where the hedge is lowest there doth every man go over" (1; Sidney, 116),[22] to distinctively Sidneian terms of phrase like the tale "able to keepe a childe from play and an old man from the chimnie corner" (8; Sidney, 113), Harington is obviously indebted to his more illustrious predecessor. Whole arguments are taken over from the *Apology,* like the assertion that poets are not liars because they do not claim that their poems are the truth (5; Sidney, 123–24). Moreover, Sidney's literary practice is drawn on to justify Ariosto's, to answer the accusation that Ariosto "breaks off narrations verie abruptly so as indeed to a loose unattentive reader will hardly carrie away any part of the storie": "If S. *Philip Sidney* had counted this a fault, he would not have done so himselfe in his Arcadia" (13).

Yet Harington's defense of poetry differs from Sidney's in important ways. Both champion poetry as a civilizing force and as a teacher of virtue, but their explanations of its workings are quite different. To the age-old problem of how the poet was at the same time to delight and to teach his audience, Harington presents a solution based on a separation of the literal, moral, and allegorical levels of the poem. Weaker readers, he says, simply enjoy the story and the verse; stronger ones appreciate the poem's moral lessons; and others more sophisticated still uncover its hidden allegorical meanings (5–6).

Sidney does not divide up the poet's audience in this way. His poet creates an ideal representation, a "speaking picture" that is almost a glimpse of the Platonic form, a golden world to "possess the sight of the soul" (101, 107). Moved by this ideal image, his readers, almost in spite of themselves, should be inspired to embrace virtue (113). He sees his poet soaring beyond nature, "freely ranging only within the zodiac of his own wit," into an unfallen perfection (100), while Harington admits freely that poetry, like philosophy, is a vanity "in respect of the high end of all, which is the health of our soules"; the best that can be said about it is that it is a watered-down divinity:

sith we live with men and not with saints and because few men can embrace this strict and stoicall divinitie . . . we do first read some other authors, making them as it were a looking glasse to the eyes of our minde, and then after we have gathered more strength, we enter into profounder studies of higher mysteries, having first as it were enabled our eyes by long beholding the sunne in a bason of water at last to looke upon the sunne it selfe. (3)

As this quotation shows, Harington's strategy is to disarm the stern critics of poetry by admitting its limitations. As to the objection that poetry contains "lightnes and wantonnes," he concedes that there is some justification for this, though "of all kinde of Poesie the Heroicall is least infected therewith" (8). Other "kindes" Harington says he will "rather excuse than defend": worst of all is "the pastorall with the Sonnet or Epigramme." His "excuse" for these are that "even the worst of them may be not ill applied and are, I must confesse, too delightfull" (9)—a sly apology, combining a casual defense on the grounds of the right use of scurrility (unspecified) and an admission of human weakness.

Sidney meets the opponents of poetry on their own ground—arguing that since the teaching of virtue is the highest aim of learning, and poetry is the best possible teacher of virtue, so it "in the most excellent work is the most excellent workman" (115). Harington, by contrast, calmly concedes that poetry's detractors are right in seeing poetry as imperfect and limited, but he reasons that since there is both profit and delight to be had from poetry, only those who refuse to admit human weakness will condemn it altogether.

Harington takes from Agrippa the four objections to poetry that form the framework for the second part of his defense (the charges that poetry is lies, that it pleases fools, breeds errors, and contains wantonness). He borrows a good deal from Sidney, as we have seen, and quotes two Martial epigrams (9). The idea of poetry as sugared medicine (3–4) he says he has taken from Tasso; the analysis he gives of the allegory of Perseus comes without acknowledgment from Leone Ebreo;[23] and the comparison of philosophy in poetry to the sun reflected in another medium derives ultimately from Plutarch.[24] Such borrowings hardly detract from the value of the preface; originality is rarely found, or even sought after, in sixteenth-century discussions of poetry. A more damaging objection is that Harington's treatment of allegory is inconsistent. The modest view of poetry as a preparation for the highest study of religion contrasts with ambitious claims about an allegorical poetry that contains a moral sense as well as the literal, and often even incorporates "some true understanding of Naturall Philosophie or somtimes of politike governement and now and then of divinitie" (5). Plutarch's view that there is a certain moral usefulness in poetry fits only approximately with Ebreo's account of the high truths concealed in the myths of the ancient poets.

The second section of Harington's preface is devoted to answering objections to *Orlando Furioso* itself. There is a general defense of the poem, based on its similarity to the *Aeneid* (a poem "allowed and approved by all men") and strengthened by the *Orlando*'s "infinit places full of Christen exhortation, doctrine, and example" of which the Pagan poet could know nothing (9–11). Then come answers to four particular objections: that the poem is lascivious, that it lacks art, and that it breaks off its narratives too abruptly and digresses too often.

It is worth quoting Harington's remarks on the salaciousness of the *Orlando Furioso,* as a sample of the nimbleness of his prose and the teasing tone that the subject prompts in him: he lists several episodes in which Ariosto is accused of being lascivious, and continues:

alas, if this be a fault, pardon him this one fault, though I doubt too many of you (gentle readers) wil be to exorable in this point, yea me thinks I see some of your searching already for these places of the booke and you are halfe offended that I have not made some directions that you might finde out and read them immediatly. But I beseech you stay a while and as the Italian saith *Pian piano,* fayre and softly, and take this caveat with you, to read them as my author ment them, to breed detestation and not delectation . . . When you read of *Alcina,* thinke how *Joseph* fled from his intising mistres . . . when on mine hostes tale (if you will follow my counsell) turne over the leafe and let it alone. . . . (11)

"Mine hostes tale" is the story of Iocondo from Book 28. Although there is a similar list of lascivious "places" in the Italian commentator Malatesta,[25] it would be surprising if any source were found for Harington's defense of them. To complete it, Harington turns to Virgil once again, claiming that the Roman poet is far franker than Ariosto, and to Chaucer, a universally respected poet who yet in-

dulged in "flat scurrilitie," not only in the Miller's Tale, but in the
Wife of Bath's Tale and many more (12).

Harington then deals with the accusation that Ariosto "wanteth
art." His discussion covers rapidly many of the points raised in the
debate among Italian critics whether *Orlando Furioso* could be ac-
commodated to the laws of epic poetry, based on Aristotle's *Poetics*
and the practice of Homer and Virgil. Some of Ariosto's defenders
claimed that his poem was not an epic at all, but was legitimate
nevertheless as an example of a modern genre, the romance, based
on a principle of variety where the epic was based on unity.[26]
Harington does not follow this line, but, drawing on various Italian
critics,[27] argues that the *Orlando* is a heroical poem, that is, an epic:

Briefly, *Aristotle* and the best censurers of Poesie, would have the *Epopeia*,
that is, the heroicall Poem, should ground on some historie and take some
short time in the same to bewtifie with his Poetrie: so doth mine Author
take the storie of K. *Charls* the great doth not exceed a yeare or thereabout
in his whole work. Secondly, they hold that nothing should be fayned
utterly incredible. And sure *Ariosto* neither in his inchantments exceedeth
credit (for who knowes not how strong the illusions of the devill are?)
neither in the miracles that *Astolfo* by the power of *S. John* is fayned to
do, since the Church holdeth that Prophetes both alive and dead have
done mightie great miracles. Thirdly, they would have an heroicall Poem
(aswell as a Tragedie) to be full of *Peripetia*, which I interpret an agnition
of some unlooked for fortune either good or bad and a sudden change
thereof: of this what store there be the reader shall quickly find. (12–13)

Some confusions are evident here.[28] The two main plot devices
Aristotle describes in the *Poetics*, discovery and reversal—what Harington calls "agnition" and "sudden change" of fortune—are mis-
leadingly combined under the term *"Peripetia,"* which belongs
properly only to the reversal of fortunes in a plot. Elsewhere, Harington cites Aristotle's axiom that poetry is an art of imitation, but
regards it (quite unlike Aristotle) as a license for the poet to create
without reference to nature: the art of poetry, Harington says, "is
but an imitation (as *Aristotle* calleth it) and therefore [poets] are
allowed to faine what they list" (4).[29]

Yet this defense of Ariosto does represent the first appearance in
English of the terms "epopeia" and "peripeteia," as the *Oxford English
Dictionary* confirms. Moreover, in the paragraph quoted above there
appear, if a little sketchily, the Aristotelian concepts of the unity

of action (the poem "should ground on some historie"), of the unity
of time (it should "take some short time in the same to beautifie
[it] with his Poetrie"), of verisimilitude ("nothing should be fayned
utterly incredible"), as well as those of discovery and reversal.

In a poem of 1593 George Peele called Harington "well letter'd
and discreet, / That hath so purely naturalized / Strange words, and
made them all free-denyzons."[30] The importance of Harington's
preface in the history of criticism is that it contains a remarkable
range of approaches, from the allegorical to the Aristotelian, organized in a loose fabric of argument about poetry in general and
one text in particular. It cannot compare with Sidney's *Apology* as
an argument, nor in its command of a critical vocabulary; it takes
its place with the rest of the *Orlando* volume as part of the ambitious
and unevenly successful enterprise of "naturalizing" not only "strange
words" but an entire critical apparatus taken from the sophisticated
world of late Renaissance Italy.

Harington's Notes and Commentary in His *Orlando*

Conventionally, the translator is a kind of ventriloquist: his own
words come from the mouth of a dummy representing the original
author. The audience is there to hear the dummy speak, and once
the performance is under way any contribution from the translator
in his own right only detracts from its authenticity. By appearing
as a commentator through an elaborate apparatus of marginal notes
alongside the text and at the end of each book, Harington contrives
to escape the limitations of the translator-ventriloquist's role and to
make a duet out of his *Orlando Furioso*. The voices are kept distinct
by a change of person: Ariosto is "I" in the text and "he" in the
marginal note beside. References to the English celebrities Hilliard
and Drake that Harington had added in early versions of the translation were in the end transferred to the notes, perhaps in deference
to this separation of the roles of translator and commentator.[31]

Occasionally Harington plays the wag to the straight man of the
text. Rinaldo calls fornication a thing "that fooles count great ex-
cesse," and Harington's note pipes up, "Wise men should count it
a greater notwithstanding good Renaldos opinion" (4.53mn). St
John waxes furious over the lack of patronage for writers in Book
35; Harington agrees that "This is belike such an offence as would

anger a Saint" (35.29mn). More often, the commentator is a kind of reader's companion. There are the occasional definitions of unfamiliar words like "mantell" or "stupendious" (29.49mn, 55mn). Gaps in the narrative are cheerfully supplied from common sense: we are not told in Book 20 how Gabrina knew Marfisa in her armor to be a woman "yet it is to be gathered that in 3 dayes companie shee might know it" (20.87mn); Ruggiero's delay in coming to the help of his king in Book 22 is not to be condemned, because he does not know what danger his master is in (22.28mn).

At times the commentary is too eager to help the reader, and works at cross-purposes with the poem itself. In his anxiety to guide the reader through the narratives, for instance, Harington names characters in the margin the instant they appear, where Ariosto delays the identification for a few stanzas. He often shortcuts Ariosto's circumlocutions by naming their subjects. Where a character disappears from the narrative, notes in the margin direct the reader to the place where he or she reappears. Harington's edition is here undoing the delicate suspensions of Ariosto's poem and unraveling the interlace of his narrative, though (according to the "Advertisement") he does appreciate the connections among Ariosto's narrative threads and means his unraveling apparatus to be used on a second reading, and then only if the reader can remember "the meane matter between the so devided stories (upon which commonly they depend)" (16).

The commentary directs the reader's appreciation of the poem as well: Harington uses it to point out the places where Ariosto shows himself most "his crafts master," as a note puts it (23.An). Very often this simply means signaling a set piece in the text, noting "simile" or "sentence" (pithy saying) in the margin, or pointing out a proverb, but occasionally he uses more recondite rhetorical terms, like "Prosopopeya" (2.29mn) or "Synonima" (5.2mn). Longer set pieces, orations like Sacripante's lamentation on Angelica's virginity, and descriptions like the one of Ruggiero as an effeminate courtier are also signaled in the margin (1.41mn, 7.46mn). Harington's index at the end of the book lists "Orations, Letters, complaints, and the like."

Another important side of the art of the poem, in Harington's eyes, is aptness in relating style to material or speaker. Olimpia's simple description of a cannon—comparing its motion and sound to wind and thunder—"doth become Olimpia well," according to

Harington's note to 9.25, "an hargabush [arquebus] being then a thing not in use." Ariosto keeps an "excellent decorum" in making Discord and Fraud of the feminine gender, while Silence is masculine (14.A). The appropriateness of the English Duke Astolfo's swearing by St. George, "after the maner of the English nobility," is noted (33.113mn).

The commentary surrounding the text in Harington's edition is used as a bridge between the world of the poem and the world of the translator and his readers. When Ariosto attacks the corruption of monasteries, for instance, Harington comments: "This reproofe is to true in most of them and hath bene sharply punished in our Realme" (14.70mn). In Book 10, Ruggiero is abused by the women of Alcina (they threaten to have him hanged in his own garters, as we have seen); Harington's "Morall" suggests that in this episode "we may observe the maner of wanton wordlings that if they see a young man live temperatly or go plainly or speake devoutly, straight they say he is a base fellow and one that knowes not what belongs to a Gentleman." Even the tale of the dog that danced and would bring anything its master asked for is neatly matched by Harington's faith in his own dog Bungey, who will stand comparison with any such animal, "onely he wants that qualitie to shake duckets out of his ears" (43.An).

Harington's aim in the commentary seems in the first instance to be to justify the poem by showing that "the ground of this Poeme is true" (1.H), that it is based on historical fact. If, on the other hand, an episode is not "true," then it must be invented; and fiction has a low status, being associated with lies, like the story of King Fieramonte and King Arthur, which "is but a fiction, for Fieramont was many yeares after Arthur" (33.7mn), or the story of Iocondo, which is "A lying tale to womens great disgrace" (28.Ar). Poetic license may go some way to justify a fiction (3.11mn), or it may be redeemed by having "allusion to some truth," such as a scriptural parallel (15.An).

Probability is the next best thing to truth in Harington's eyes; it is not necessary in Ricciardetto's tale to Fiordispina, which is "a frivolus tale, devised by him to blear her eys" (25.51mn), but the tale of the enchanted cup must be true or probable if it is to have any force of argument (43.M). Some justification may also be found in the valuable observations to be drawn from the invented part of the poem; in "the great likenes of face of [the twins] *Bradamant* and

Richardetto," for example, "(though this be but a fiction) yet we
may observe the rare and (as it were) cunning workmanship of
nature" (25.M).

Where these justifications are not appropriate—where an episode
is obviously fabulous—Harington often offers allegory as the proper
way to understand the poem. At the beginning of canto 7, Ariosto
glances at those who might not believe in his fantastic creation,
comparing them to the simple people who will only believe what
they can see and touch for themselves. Harington ignores the ironic
implications of this and suggests in his marginal gloss that Ariosto's
tale will seem a mere fable only to those who miss its allegory
(7.1mn).

Allegory has aroused a particular dislike among critics committed
to the idea that letter and spirit are indissolubly bound together in
literature. A famous instance is Benedetto Croce's attack on the
allegorizers of Dante's *Divine Comedy*. Croce argued that allegory
could only be joined to poetry *ab extra,* as an arbitrary equivalence
between elements in it and an element in the world outside it, or
could itself occupy the place of poetry, as "a crowd of discordant
images, poetically frigid and mute." In the first case, the poetry
remains intact, though in terms of allegorical interpretation it is
"simply an object serving as a sign"; in the second, the images of
poetry are replaced by mere signs, and only "nothingness and ug-
liness" remains.[32]

A similar feeling that allegorical interpretation is essentially anti-
poetical lies behind the doubts of modern critics that such interpretations can be a true reflection of the way the interpreter reads
the text. R. E. Neil Dodge suggested that Harington's commentary
on Ariosto falls into the critical dualism of the Italians who "read
and enjoy the poem one way and interpret it another." Townsend
Rich maintained that Spenser cast Ariosto's material into the allegorical mold "sincerely and all too ardently," while Harington did
so "playfully and expediently"; the notes in his *Orlando,* like the
preface, "were probably written to forestall critics of the [Puritan]
school of Gosson and Stubbes."[33]

It is impossible to know Harington's motives in constructing the
critical apparatus for his *Orlando Furioso.* In cases like the tale of
Ricciardetto and Fiordispina, where he announces that he is aiming
to "temper" or at least "salve" lascivious matters, we may suspect
that his moralizing interpretation is mere ingenuity (25.M). Where

he is borrowing allegorical interpretations holus-bolus from one of his sources, as in the "Allegorie" to Book 4, it may be mainly a matter of filling up a page of his carefully organized volume.[34]

Yet most of Harington's allegorizing does not fall into the sort of critical dualism that has been suggested. On the whole, he does not resort to allegory to explain away scurrility in the text: he is more likely to shake his head in mock horror at such things, as he does in the "Allusion" to Book 28, or to suggest (in effect) that to the pure all things are pure, as with the embraces of Ruggiero and Alcina (7.27mn). An exception is Angelica's love-idyll with Medoro, ending with their marriage: Harington says, in the "Allegorie" to Book 19, "*Angelica* is taken for honor, which brave men hunt after by blood and battells and many hardie feats and misse it, but a good servant with faith and gratefulnesse to his Lord gets it"; an interpretation that is, as Paul J. Alpers notes, "at least in the spirit of the episode."[35]

Moreover, the allegories Harington suggests are on the whole not abstract, secret meanings but the kind of conclusions any reader might draw: not cryptic messages encoded by the author in his fiction but a matter for pleasurable, even fanciful consideration by the audience. This is the "Allegorie" to Book 29, dealing with Isabella's strategy to outwit Rodomonte:

Some perhaps will pike a pretie Allegorie in the confection that *Isabella* made, and indeed it is a pretie receit if it be well marked . . . an herbe . . . mingled with elder berryes and rew (which may signifie sage counsell and repentance), and strayned between harmles hands, which betokens innocencie, boyled on a fire of Cypres, which the auncient Romanes used at funeralls and therefore may be taken either for death or persecution or martyrdome: this confection used in due order will be a good Antidoton or medicine against fire and sword; under which is signified all the perils and adversities of the world.

Most of the allegories Harington deals with in his notes concern supernatural, magical, or simply marvelous objects, events, and figures. In Book 20, for instance, which deals with the escape from the island of the Amazons by means of the magic horn and Zerbino's punishment for mocking Gabrina, Harington concludes that "All the Allegoricall matter . . . is onely in *Astolfos* horne" (20.A). The idea that the marvels of romance were allegorical was well established in Italian critics in the last quarter of the sixteenth century. In fact, it was felt that the marvelous scenes, which symbolized unseen processes, were what made epic and romance philosophical. In this, Renaissance interpreters were following the Greek tradition that allegorized Homer's gods and goddesses, dealing at one stroke with Plato's objections that poetry contained scurrilous tales about the gods and that it told untruths. They considered that the fabulous heroes and heroines and the magical weapons and adornments of the romances signaled the presence of allegory, as the superhuman power and the elaborate accessories of the gods did in Homer.[36]

As well as the allegory of the marvelous, the Italian commentators like Fornari found in Ariosto "continued allegory," in the phrase familiar from Spenser's letter to Raleigh about *The Faerie Queene.* This consisted of abstract equivalents for recurrent characters, animals, or objects in the poem that were not necessarily fabulous. Harington's notes do include allegories of this type, mostly (but not all) borrowed from his reading in the Italian commentators. He says in the "Allegorie" to Book 1 that Baiardo, Rinaldo's horse, represents man's ungovernable desires; Ruggiero's troubled courtship of Bradamante he says shows man's struggle against bodily and spiritual enemies to gain true contentment in the world (44.A); and he suggests that the fact that Ruggiero kills Rodomonte immediately after marrying Bradamante is an allegory of the furious passions of youth being "killed and quite vanquished" by marriage (46.A). The "Briefe and Summarie Allegorie" at the end of Harington's book, translated for the most part from its equivalent in Fornari's edition, gives an extended allegorical interpretation of the Ruggiero-Alcina episode (559-64). In general, however, Harington puts these more abstract interpretations forward with some hesitation, disdaining the excesses of searching out an allegory "where none is intended by the Author him selfe" (1.A), and acknowledging that his allegory for the island of Ebuda in Book 11 may seem "greatly strayned" to some.[37]

Harington's commentary is not a mechanical exercise in fanciful allegory intended to placate the moralists; in Croce's terms, he does not treat the text "simply as an object serving as a sign," but attends closely to its pleasures, its effects, and its implications. At its best, Harington's commentary conveys a lively response to the text which is also a morally directed one. There is no sense that he is reading and enjoying the poem one way and interpreting it in another. While the allegorical theory of his preface suggests a view of the poet as inspired prophet veiling the truth in poetry, Harington's practice in his commentary on Ariosto is closer to a model of the poet as providing exemplary fictions, striking images of virtue or vice; this brings him nearer to Sidney and the more modern mimetic theory than might appear from the preface alone.[38] Harington's moderate approach to allegory avoids the implication that allegorical meanings are arbitrarily connected to the signs constituted by surface narrative elements; his approach is more properly moralizing rather than allegorizing. By this method, the importance of the events and characters in the poem is preserved: it leads the reader to inspect them carefully for the lesson they can offer. The integrity of the sign, the poetry, is thus safeguarded.

In the notes a wide variety of matters is dealt with which cannot be classified as literary-critical commentary on the poem. There is, for example, the makings of a treatise on statesmanship, a treatise that would have been a rebuttal of Machiavelli's *The Prince,* based on Christian principles in place of Machiavelli's pragmatism. Harington notes, for instance, that King Norandino's generosity in Book 18, in making Grifone amends for having mistakenly reviled him, goes against "that heathnish (nay divelish) saying of *Machiavell* that whom you have done a great injurie to, him you must never pardon but still persecute . . . how far is this doctrine from his that taught to forgive not seven times but seaventie times seaven times?" (18.M). An example to be avoided is Ludovico Sforza, mentioned in Book 33, "the notablest dissembler and Machiavillian that ever was, though before Machiavels time," according to Harington's notes, habitually "plotting of new devises to set other Princes at variaunce . . . taking part with one side openlie and feeding the other with money secretlie" (33.28mn, H). Elsewhere, Harington's commentary offers pithy observation on the people's hatred for princes' favorites (17.70mn), on the costliness of keeping a royal army (38.H), on the mutability of Fortune and the folly of relying on others' protection (40.M).

The bounty of princes is a special hobby-horse of Harington's. A shrewd comment in the "Morall" to Book 34 suggests that princes should not expect their subjects to put up with ingratitude or injury, for it is in the nature of man and especially "of brave and resolut minded men," to seek revenge when they think themselves "disdayned or their services not well regarded." The prince will do well to remember that "love and bountie are stronger bands of allegeance then fear and duetie."

Harington's *Orlando* is an enterprise in practical and theoretical criticism with no equal in Elizabethan letters. It has, however, been hard to take it seriously, in his own time and since. The traditional story of its origins as a salacious court tidbit has already been told; there is no doubt that Harington gives full play to its sexual elements in the published version, in his illustrations as well as in the text.

Modern readers, as we have seen, have for several reasons tended to treat Harington's apparatus as a sport, either ironically intended or merely derivative. Such a response is less than fair to Harington's efforts to define the proper degree of seriousness with which Ariosto's poem should be treated. Two main instances are the problem of the lascivious episodes and the general problem of fiction itself: in both, Harington defines his position in relation to a puritanical viewpoint, one that would condemn lasciviousness in literature as leading souls into damnation by encouraging immorality and condemn fiction outright as lies. Harington's response to the first is mixed. He makes the most of the enjoyable innuendoes of the lascivious parts of the text, and he accepts that such passages are part of the pleasure of reading. On the other hand, he does not dismiss moralizing objections to them. His instinct is to be tolerant; his view of the fallible nature of readers—that they are mere men, not saints—leads him to reject overrigid, "stoicall" censurers of their texts as inevitably hypocritical. Nevertheless, he concedes something of the strength of their position, and marshals his apologetic arguments fairly casually. He defines a tolerant, antihypocritical attitude to the problem, rather than offering a solution.

On the question of fiction his view is a curious contrast to Ariosto's. The irony of *Orlando Furioso* is elastic and elusive: the more the poet protests his innocence and presents his authentications, the more the reader is made to recognize the illusion in which he is participating. Harington, as commentator, examines the poem first of all to verify it as history. His skepticism is brought into play only because he takes the text as evidence seriously. Where the poem cannot be history, it must be fiction; and for Harington, fiction is not play but a challenge, a diversion from the truth for which justification must be found. Probable fictions, for example, are shown in Harington's commentary to provide a moral, or striking images of virtue and vice, or illustrations of the consequences of

good and bad deeds. Improbable elements may be explained either
as "strange reports" from far-off places, which the reader should not
dismiss too readily (as in Harington, 2.54, where Atlante fights a
battle on the winged horse), or as allegories. The idea of a pure
fiction—a delightful illusion to be enjoyed for its own sake, which
might seem more in the spirit of Ariosto himself—is not considered.

Harington's brand of seriousness aims to moralize without hypocrisy, and to test the text earnestly for its truthfulness and coax
out its moral lessons while responding to its imaginative vigor. It
was an unstable mixture: for the modern reader, it falls in an awkward gap between Ariosto's sophisticated, endlessly elastic irony
about his poem and the more radical skepticism of present-day
attitudes to literary texts. In Harington's own day, likewise, it fell
in an awkward middle ground between aristocratic moral laxity—
the truculent atheism and hedonism represented by men like Raleigh—and the self-righteous moral severity of the "strict and
stoicall."

Aeneid, Book 6

Harington's translation of Book 6 of the *Aeneid*[39] is a workmanlike
performance, maintaining a bold narrative outline, rendering direct
speech plainly and effectively, while passing over some of the in-
tricacies of narrative and descriptive detail. As a sample of the verse,
here is the meeting between Aeneas and Dido in the Underworld
in Harington's version:

> Heer wofull Dydo late arryv'd did rawnge,
> in that wyld wood with wownd yet fresh to see,
>   Her good Eneas did agnyze eftsoone,
>   by glims of lyght moche lyke the rysing moone.
>
> Endeerd with sweet compassyon thus hee spake
> alasse and was the news I hard so trew,
> fayr Queen, that thow didst suffer for my sake,
> wo mee was I of death of cawse to yow?
> how loth was I thy sweetnes to forsake?
> by heavns I swear, or yf that fayth bee dew
>   to othes in place heer of Infernall ghosts,
>   full sore agaynst my will I left yo*u*r coasts.
>
> But I constrayned was by heavnly hest,
> by Joves expresse and unresysted will,

which brings mee now to place of restlesse rest,
by help of strawnge and unacquainted skill,
nor cold I (to say trewly) once have gest
yow cold have tane my parting halfe so yll.
   Why shunne yow mee? oh heer mee I beseech,
   tis fate that geves mee leave to use this speech.

Thus good Eneas spake with moystned ey
with tender talke to mitygat her moan,
she sullen sylent maketh no reply,
but stood lyke statue wrowght of Marble stone;
at last in great dispyte shee thence doth fly
to next adioyning woods, and thear anon
   among the shades obskure of mirtle bows,
   shee meets Sychews her fyrst loved spows.

This accydent did greeve Eneas moste
Yet followd still her syght till trees did barre. . . .
                              (stanzas 66–70)

The emphatic final couplets give a certain robustness; Aeneas's plea to Dido has an authentic plaintiveness ("Why shunne yow me? oh hear me I beseech"); when the time comes to move the narrative along, as in stanza 69 ("Thus good Eneas spake with moystned ey"), it is briskly done. Harington has thirty lines to Virgil's twenty-seven (11. 450–76); in fact, this represents a certain compression given the density of the original and the demands of his *ottava rima* form. What is lost by this compression can be seen in Virgil's comparison of Dido's being no more moved by Aeneas's plea "quam si dura silex aut stet Marpesia cautes" ("than if she were set in hard flint or Marpesian rock," 1. 471),[40] which becomes "lyke statue wrowght of Marble stone" (st. 69), cursory if not exactly inaccurate. The comparison of Aeneas's first sight of Dido to a fleeting, uncertain glimpse of the new moon among clouds, "qualem primo qui surgere mense / aut videt aut vidisse putat per nubila lunam" ("even as, in the early month, one sees or fancies he has seen the moon rise amid the clouds," 11. 453–54), is diminished to a brief simile for the light by which Aeneas recognizes Dido, a glimmer "moche lyke the rysing moone" (st. 66).

There is interpolation as well as repetition: Aeneas's elaboration of his present mission, sent "per loca senta situ . . . noctemque profundam" ("through lands squalid and forsaken, and through abysmal night," 1. 462) is omitted and we have a new and distracting idea that Aeneas has come "by help of strawnge and unacquainted skill" (st. 68). Occasionally Harington seems to have failed entirely to negotiate his original; "extremum fato, quod te adloquor, hoc est" ("The last word Fate suffers me to say to thee is this!" 1. 466) is rendered inaccurately as "tis fate that geves mee leave to use this speech" (st. 68). (This makes for an awkward repetition of the topic of the means by which Aeneas has come to the Underworld.) In stanza 70, the detail that Aeneas followed the fleeing form of Dido "till trees did barre" is Harington's own.

A second brief quotation from the translation will help to show Harington's competence at rendering the more formal structures of the original. This is from Virgil's description of the Elysian fields:

> hic manus ob patriam pugnando volnera passi,
> quique sacerdotes casti, dum vita manebat,
> quique pii vates et Phoebo digna locuti,
> inventas aut qui vitam excoluere per artis,
> quique sui memores aliquos fecere merendo:
> omnibus his nivea cinguntur tempora vitta.

(Here is the band of those who suffered wounds, fighting for fatherland; those who in lifetime were priests and pure, good bards, whose songs were meet for Phoebus; or they who ennobled life by truths discovered and they who by service have won remembrance among men—the brows of all bound with snowy fillet.) (6:660–65)

Harington has

> Heer sowldyers stowt that fowght for cowntrys laws
> heer preests that follow prayr with chast intentions
> heer Poets uttring phebus sacred saws,
> heer those that ayd mankynde with good inventions,
> or meryt poor mens prayr, and help theyr cawse.
> all clothd in whyte receaved eternall pencyons.
>
>   (st. 98)

He has made something very much his own out of Virgil's list: we recognize the voice of the veteran of the Irish wars in the commendation of "sowldyers stowt," of the opinionated churchman in

the reference to the "chast intentions" that must follow the priests'
prayers, of the designer of the metamorphosed Ajax in the reference
to "those that ayd mankynde with good inventions" and of the
lifelong courtier in the "eternall pencyons" received by these fortunate beings.

Harington quotes these lines in his "Epistle" to King James at
the beginning of the Reading manuscript of the translation, and
confesses "that evn to this howr reeding this fabulows narracion of
the Elisyan feelds I take a comfort for the tyme, and ymagin that
by one of those tytles I may one day challenge a walke in those
feelds of which hee wrytes." It is the account of heaven and hell in
Book 6 that makes it so suitable for Prince Henry, Harington says;
moreover, no poet better than Virgil, and no book of Virgil's better
than this one "sets foorth and commends the piety of a sonne to
his parent."

As in his *Orlando Furioso,* Harington's notes to Virgil are varied
and individual. He points out curiosities, explains proper names,
places and characters, commends particular instances of appropriateness in the original, and explains certain facets of the translation.
There is even a little historical criticism—the lamentation for Mar-
cellus's death is "in a fashion so pleasing to the humor of those
tymes" that Octavia gave the poet more than a thousand pounds
for it ([88,90]). There is a reference, reminiscent of the *Orlando*
commentary, to the respect earned by the religious prince ([82]).
Ariosto's poem is clearly still on the mind of the Harington of 1604
writing the notes. He indicates the places where Ariosto had imitated Virgil, and on some occasions notes his opinion that Ariosto
has outstripped the Roman poet: Virgil's description of Elysium
"fayls evn in the fyrst glory which showld bee the lyght, which hee
calls heer a purple lyght":

hee wrytes of yt as yf he wear but in Campo Marcio to see men at pastymes
thear . . . yf I bee not Parciall, the place Aryosto discrybes ys far more
sutable for a paradyce then this thowgh hee allows not so moche company. . . . (64, 66)

The burning question for Harington in this book of the *Aeneid*
is how Virgil's picture of heaven and hell matches an acceptable
Christian one. Harington notes how reward and punishment are
meted out in Virgil's system. The lustful Pasiphae rightly suffers

in the hell reserved for those who died for love, according to Harington, but Euadne and Laodamia, who died of grief for lost husbands, "yf I had been Mynos [president of the court of Hell] showld have had a better place then Pasyphae" (46). Soldiers who are wounded in the service of their country, "with a very good decorum" are placed in the Elysian fields (68), and swaggering camp-followers (like Sir John Falstaff) are condemned to hell (48). He is interested that the damned are not in such extreme torment that they cannot reason and discourse (50).

In this fascination with the pagan version of heaven and hell, the key concept is the "light of nature."[41] Virgil, in Harington's note, "shows what opinion the Pagans had by instinct of nature, of punishment after his lyfe according to the quallyty of theyr offences" ([76]). He notes how the fall of the giants who attempted to overthrow Jupiter resembles the fall of the rebel angels (60); the pagan Fates resemble the Christian idea of Predestination (38); he notes that "the number of the elect are but few even in the pagans opinion" ([76]). At times, as St. Augustine points out, Virgil "speaks not only Christianlyke but evn lyke Chryst him selfe" (68).

In the essays added at the end of the translation—provided, Harington says, to treat fully the matters for which there was not enough space in the notes—these problems are raised once again. Harington says he is seeking a middle way between the ever-present danger that the young reader may "fall into error, eyther by geving credyt to them to moche to grow supersticiows or by utter reiectinge them as meer fyctions to grow alltogether carelesse and Incredulows." A distinction between matters of faith, which are indisputable, and matters of reason, which may be discussed (though without "presumption and parcialyty"), provides a preliminary guide ([93–94]). That the latter is the greater danger Harington is in no doubt: "I wold rather my sonnes showld beleeve all the old tales of Purgatory and Lymbus, then thinke that thear ys not a hell whear sinners shalbee punished" ([117]).

The general problem of a proper faith, steering a middle course between the Scylla of superstition and the Charybdis of atheism, is bound up with the problem of the truth of poetry. On the one hand, Harington gives as the first rule for the reader of poetry to remember that poets feign—that is, they are liars. As he says in the notes on Hercules' visit to Hell, "Poets so wrye the trewth with fables & storyes with allegoryes that no great heed ys to be taken of them" (18). Armed with this knowledge, the reader of poetry must be an active interpreter, always ready to winnow "truth from the fable the veryty from the vanytye"; when a passion is described, he should not sympathize with it but "moralyce the fiction to discover whear the fawlt ys" ([152–53]).

Such rules demand a vigilant skepticism in the reader of poetry. On the other hand, the reader should not simply dismiss poetry because it is feigned: in the case of Virgil's account of Aeneas's journey to the underworld, for instance, though "the lytterall & historycall sence ys meerly and apparawntly fabulows, yet the morall thearof contayns so many excellent points of Christiantye" ([107]). The proper suspicions of the reader of poetry must be controlled, therefore, and Harington warns of the dangers of an unrestrained skepticism, like that of the modern Hebraists who say that hell itself "ys but meer poetry" ([111]). God forbid, Harington says, that

a trew Christian, that reeds in Ovids Metamorphosis Lycaon turnd into a Wolfe and Niobe into a stone, both w*h*ich are fyctions, showld thearfore dowbt of the veryty of the sacred History, Whear yt ys written how Lotts wyfe by a powrfull Metamorphosis, was turnd into a salt stone. . . . ([156])

Harington warns that poetry is limited and cannot represent things that are by definition beyond mortal apprehension, like the joys of heaven, of which St. Paul "sayth the Ey hath not seen nor the ear herd nor hath yt enterd into the hart of man, What god hath prepared for those that Love him" ([155]). He says earlier in his notes that Virgil makes his Elysian fields too much like the Campus Martius; Ariosto does better and St. John better still in Revelations in describing heaven, but even St. John's "walls of preciows stons gates of Perle & ryvers of Cristall" are "things subiect to owr understanding," when (again quoting Paul) no mortal can know what is in store for the elect (66).

The last of Harington's essay commentaries is on the subject "Of reeding poetry." The attitude he expresses to poetry is a wary one: the rules he is to present are *"Antidotons"* against the infection in some poetry; on the whole, he thinks that more harm than good is done to young men by reading poetry, because their minds are readier to accept bad influence than good, and because bad writers

are more numerous than good ([148]). Nevertheless, he says that
while "I wold cownt them to lyght that wold wholly apply them
selves to nothing but poetry, so I iudg them to stryct that wold
have poetry excluded from a yowng mans studyes." Poetry is like

a concubyn that a man in his fancy, in wyne and myrth, and wanton
company, embraces and calls the Joy of his lyfe, but retyred in his sober
thowghts, and with his trew frends cold wysh they had been lesse ac-
quaynted with her and sooner left her. . . . ([149])

As in the notes to *Orlando,* Harington moralizes rather than al-
legorizes the *Aeneid.* There is no allegory for Aeneas's descent into
hell, like the ones Harington's predecessors had supplied (Landino,
for instance, describes the descent as the mind's investigation of
man's sensual condition).[42] In Harington's eyes, the gods and legends of antiquity were metaphors rather than allegories:[43] Pluto was
probably a rich prince (18); the flight of Icarus was a ship's voyage,
ships' sails being called wings by metaphor ([6]).

Harington emerges from his commentaries as an enthusiastic par-
tisan of his chosen authors; he examines their texts with earnest
interest for answers to the burning questions of his own day. He
assumes that the reader of such texts must be an active one—
discriminating between history and fiction, alerted by fiction to a
moral significance and by the fabulous to allegory. He regards texts
as powerful—like the *Aeneid,* they may provoke questions that will
lead the unprepared to atheism and damnation, but they may also
inspire the godly and terrify the wicked: the "whole dryft" of Book
6 is to show

that the vallor and Pyety of Eneas overcame all the difficultyes not only
of earth but of hell, and ys rewarded, with prosperows successe, a fayr
wyfe, a gloryows posteryty, and at last with immortalytye; and yet by the
way, towches the damnacion and torments, of giants and Tyrants, and all
manner of Malefactors, that a good mynde allmost may bee edyfyed, and
an yll mynde, yf not rectyfyed, yet terrefyed by his wrytings. ([153])

Harington also responded enthusiastically to the pathos in his authors; in the "Moral" to Book 24 of *Orlando* he remarks that the
tragical end of Isabella and Zerbino is "set downe by my author in
a sort to move so great compassion that it seems all that read it are

as it were in love with them and lament their so unfortunate end," and he confesses that it was only the fear of "wronging mine author" that stopped him changing the poem to give their lives a happier ending.

In *A Preface to Chaucer,* D. W. Robertson, Jr., places the poet in a tradition of open-minded and optimistic readers, beginning with the Church Fathers and surviving into the Christian Humanists of the early Renaissance.[44] They sought to find good moral instruction in secular and even in pagan literature, in spite of the conventional hostility to the frivolities and heresies in such works. Harington's commentaries belong in this Humanist tradition, which aspired to a philosophy of serious joking and studious playing. A degree of skepticism and an orthodox caution about doctrine show that he also responded to the dogmatically serious atmosphere of his own age; but such doubts did not prevail in the end over his irrepressible enthusiasm for the pleasures and uses of literature.

Chapter Three
The Metamorphosis of Ajax

Harington's book is in three parts, *A New Discourse of a Stale Subject, called the Metamorphosis of Ajax, An Anatomie of the Metamorpho-sed Ajax,* and *An Apologie.* They were published as a unit in the first edition, but the *New Discourse* and the *Anatomie* (the latter probably with the *Apologie*) were issued separately in 1596 as well.[1] The title puns on the Elizabethan word for the privy—jakes—and the "metamorphosis" referred to is Harington's improvement of the device to include a flush and a seal.

The *New Discourse* starts with a letter from "Philostilpnos" ("lover of cleanliness"), Harington's cousin Edward Sheldon.[2] It urges Harington to publish his invention, notwithstanding the homeliness of the subject. Harington's reply, signed "Misacmos" ("hater of filth"), elaborates on the usefulness of the reformed privy and the propriety of writing about it. A "Prologue" follows, giving various fantastical etymologies for the term "jakes." Harington's punning, allusive, scurrilous stories intertwine the Greek hero Ajax and Rabelais's Gargantua, and he manages to include a hymn to Satan in monks' Latin and a final metaphor of the smell of the privy as Ajax's foul breath.

The main part of the *New Discourse* is a mixture of seriousness and merriment, as its "Short Advertisement" says. It aims first to justify "the use of the homelyest wordes," then to prove "the matter not to be contemptible," and finally to describe the present state of domestic sanitation and what can be done about it, "the forme, and how it may be reformed" (81). The list of contents prepares the reader for the play of ironies in what is to follow: Harington's terminology brings into conjunction the humble subject of the privy and the grand scholastic division between matter and form, and hints at a parallel between the ecclesiastical Reformation and the reformation of the privy.

The first part of the *New Discourse* shows how "homely" words have been used "without reproofe of ribaldrie, or scurrilitie" in "writings both holy, and prophane, Emblemes, Epigrams, Histories, and ordinarie and familiar communication" (110). To demonstrate that in the past the authorities took the problems of sanitation seriously, there are examples in the second part from the Bible as well as from Roman history. At one point, Harington imagines himself to be the Emperor Vespasian's secretary, and writes a mock edict on the erection of public urinals in "faire polished marble" (126–28)—a good instance of the exuberant variations he plays on his theme.

In the last section of the *New Discourse,* Harington describes how even in the best houses in the land, "notwithstanding all our provisions of vaults, of sluces, of grates, of paines of poor folkes in sweeping and scouring," there is still "this same whorson sawcie stinke," penetrating to the innermost sanctum of "the faire Ladies chambers" (160). Various solutions and their drawbacks are discussed, Harington's device is proposed, and the circumstances of its invention described. Before taking leave of the reader he defends himself once again, against the charges of being fantastical, of being scurrilous, and of being satirical.

In the *Anatomie,* as Harington promises at the end of the *New Discourse,* his servant Thomas Combe describes the device and its construction in detail, with illustrations. Combe's subtitle shows how far he follows his master in amplifying the topic at hand: in his section

BY A TRIPERTITE METHOD is plainly, openly, and demonstratively, declared, explained, and eliquidated, by pen, plot and precept, how unsaverie places may be made sweet, noysome places made wholesome, filthie places made cleanly. (187)

He joins battle once again with those who would accuse the book of scurrility, offering two syllogisms on the use of homely words in "necessary matters" (201).

The last part of the book, the *Apologie,* takes as its pretext a dream in which a visitor tells the writer of a group of gentlemen who settled down to read his book after dinner, intrigued by its title. Shocked to find the book more satirical than obscene, they decide to arraign the author on ten charges, ranging from idleness to knavish attacks on the authorities. Twelve jurymen are called, twelve of Harington's friends, who are named and described at length. Finally, the charges against the book are brought and discharged.

With that, the writer awakes from his dream and vows never to write "any more such idle toys, if this were well taken" (265).

The *Metamorphosis* is a discourse on privies and excretion, arranged in an elaborate scheme of three parts, themselves divided into internal sections. It contains a wildly miscellaneous collection of learning, observation, and gossip. In the middle is the design for a modified privy, with working diagrams; around it are layers of explanation, apology, self-defense, and discussion of terms. The whole is perhaps most like a fantastic court hearing: a gallimaufry of documents, arguments, submissions, and learned pleading—a cornucopia of rhetoric—all returning, eventually, to the subject of the hearing, the privy.

The Reformed Privy as an Invention

Remarks in letters and epigrams show that Harington actually "reformed" some privies, at Richmond Palace and other great houses as well as at Kelston.[3] His device involves a flushing system, drawing on a cistern, and an inner "stool pot" emptied and sealed by a plunger-type stopper. An historian of sanitation, Ernest Sabine, calls it "the first crude valve water-closet," "the beginning of the modern valve water-closet with its temporary receptacle, or bowl, now flushed and refilled with water each time that it is used."[4]

The medieval privy was essentially a hole over a pit. In great houses or castles the "garderobes" were built within the walls, with a vertical shaft below a stone or wooden seat. Arrangements for the "rere-dorters" of the monasteries were similar. If possible, the pit underneath was drained by a diverted stream or even by the tide; otherwise, cesspools had to be emptied at regular intervals by "gong-farmers" who made their living this way. In London, the Thames and other water-courses provided convenient drainage. Sabine says that the better-off usually tried to reduce the stench by having chamber and cesspool connected only by pipe; the rest of the population used privies placed directly over the cesspool, with only a floor between.[5]

The history of improvements to this basic form is untidy. In medieval times there are a few instances of water-flushing from above, using stone or lead cisterns filled with rainwater.[6] Early in the sixteenth century, Leonardo designed a castle for Francis I of France, including "a large number of closets, all on the same side of the castle, connected together and provided with flushing channels inside the walls and ventilating shafts reaching up to the roof."[7] According to Lawrence Wright, the medieval garderobe was not built in sixteenth-century houses, and its place was taken by the "close stool," whose contents had to be removed by the servants.[8]

Harington's invention is thus a considerable advance. It did not lead to any permanent improvement in sanitation, however. For one thing, Harington was mainly concerned with odors, with "reforming Maister Ajax ill breath," rather than with hygiene. Moreover, as Henry E. Sigerist comments in an article on the subject, the water closet "could not come into more general use before houses were supplied with running water and connected with sewers . . . centuries had to elapse before medicine could demonstrate the necessity of plenty of fresh water and of a quick removal of sewage."[9] There is no record of any general adoption of Harington's device. The existence of a flushing system in a Surrey house in 1654 is remarkable enough for John Aubrey to record it in his papers;[10] through the eighteenth century, the water closet remained something of a novelty, even in great houses. Late in the century, the first patents were taken out for water closets with a flushing system and valves. The modern form dates from about 1889.[11]

Harington's proposal for a reformed privy was embedded in an elaborately ironic, satiric, and metaphoric structure, a display of fantastic learned wit. The inventor Hugh Plat was one of those who found Harington's presentation objectionable. At the end of a pamphlet called *Sundrie new and Artificiall remedies against Famine* he refers specifically to the *Metamorphosis:*

that I could fal into M. *Ajax* veine, and had some of his glib paper, & gliding pens, I might soon scribble ten sheets, and sell everie sheet for two pence, towarde necessarie charges: and in the end conclude the expectation of manie leaves, in a few sweeter lines than he hath done before me: but because I bind my selfe to no such privy presidents, I will deliver my conceipt in as plain and naked tearmes as I may.[12]

The exchange had begun with a lively section in the *Metamorphosis* satirizing Plat's aspirations to profitable patents and monopolies. The reformed privy is a satiric touchstone: Harington connects Plat's newly invented coal-balls with his own device—the former, he suggests, may use the by-products of the latter in their recipe.

Moreover, he proposes that he and Plat should join forces: Harington will apply for the exclusive right to set up public privies in London and to charge a fee each time they are used (making him the richest squire in London); and he offers to write a petition for a monopoly for Plat on coal-balls, urging that iron mills and glass works must continue, showing that this will mean the destruction of still more forests for their furnaces and so proving that the new fuel is more than ever essential to the economy (166–68).

Harington fastened on what was undoubtedly a ridiculous side to Plat's endeavors, namely a coyness about his inventions and about the fact that he wanted to sell his discoveries. Nevertheless, Plat was an authentic pioneer in scientific and technical investigation, "the most resourceful patentee of his generation"; even the coal-balls are taken seriously by historians of science.[13] His principles are those of Francis Bacon and the founders of the Royal Society: he champions modern civilization against the ancient, claiming that the ancients allowed theory to overrule practice. He remarks that some of them, ignoring "the infallible grounds of practise, have published whole Volumes by imagination onely." Moreover, they are obscure because they have described their experiments "so figurativelie, and wrapped them up in such clouds of skill."[14]

It was the discrepancy in Harington's *New Discourse* between prolix introduction and meager practical exposition that Plat attacked, contrasting it with his own "plain and naked terms." Plat must have seen Harington as the representative of an outmoded humanism, idolizing the ancients, obscuring his message with copious allusions, digressions, and elaborations, a theorist who clouded matters of practical utility with learned irony. Plat belonged to the developing commercial world of patents and monopolies. Harington chose to satirize Plat's clumsy attempts to advertise himself and turn his "secrets" into profit; his own invention was given to the world in a showcase so elaborate that its usefulness seems to have been the last thing its readers noticed.

The *Metamorphosis* as Satire

Harington's Elizabethan readers must have seen the *Metamorphosis* first of all as a controversial pamphlet. Thomas Nashe's first reaction when he read it was that it was pure scatology. In a letter written in the summer vaction of 1596, he notes that all is quiet in London,

Only mr Harrington [of] late hath sett vp sutch filthy stinking iakes in pouls [ch]urchyard, that the stationers wold give any mony for a couer [fo]r it. What shold moue him to it I know not, except he [m]eant to bid a turd in all gentle readers teeth. . . .[15]

In *Have With You to Saffron Walden* (1596) Nashe can think of no better epithets for the Harvey brothers than "the most contemptible *Mounsier Ajaxes* of excrementall conceipts and stinking kennel-rakt up invention."[16]

"Misodiaboles," the anonymous author of *Ulysses upon Ajax,* a pamphlet that followed the *Metamorphosis* into print in 1596, was in no doubt about Harington's motives: "from the meanes of a privie, he will become a publicke gentleman." Misodiaboles pictures Harington as frustrated to see his *Orlando Furioso* fail—he says it was condemned officially for its bawdiness, and elsewhere for its "barrain & servile" translation—while the world was "so full of good wittes generallie redde and applauded." In malcontented humor, Misodiaboles says, Harington "in steade of a wittie treatise, hath turnde me out to light his unfavored *Ajax.*" Harington had abandoned proper decorum and changed a "courteors habite" for a "fooles antique" and has become a jester, a spectacle of folly.[17]

In a letter of August 1596, already quoted, Harington confesses that the *Metamorphosis* was an exercise in controversy, a calculated publicity stunt. Buried in the country too long, he wished to have himself talked about, and (in what seems to have been a disastrous miscalculation) to show himself worthy of service with his pen or otherwise to his prince and country.[18]

Within the *Metamorphosis,* Harington anticipated the accusation that his book is merely a piece of fooling meant to attract attention. One of the charges against him he reports in the *Apologie* is that because he realized that these days "even at wise mens tables, fooles have most of the talke," he has taken up a fool's bauble to have his tale heard. To this he pleads guilty (212). In answering objections to the unworthy subject he has chosen in the *Metamorphosis,* he asks

If I had entituled the booke, *A Sermon shewing a soveraigne salve for the sores of the soule.* Or, *A wholsome haven of health to harbour the heart in.* Or, *A marvellous medicine for the maladies of the minde.* would you ever have asked after such a booke? would these grave and sober titles have wonne you to the view of three or foure tittles? much lesse three or foure score periodes. But when you heard, there was one had written of A Jax, straight you had a great mind to see what strange discourse it would prove, you made enquirie who wrote it, where it might be had, when it wold come forth . . . you hoped for some meriments, some toyes, some scurrilitie, or to speake plaine English, some knaverie. (181)

He goes on to claim that the reader has swallowed all sorts of health-giving pills disguised in his entertaining confection. These pills he calls "the true intent of the booke" (182, n. q). In the prologue and first part of the *New Discourse* they consist of attacks on "malcontents, Epicures, Atheists, heretickes, & carelesse & dissolute Christians, and especially against pride and sensualitie." There is indeed mild satire of these categories in the sections referred to, in the description of Ajax as a "perfit mal-content" (67), the jibe at those who avoid saying "amen" when the commandment against adultery is read in church (84), and the story of the heretic Arrius, who died on the privy (92). Presumably the contrasts of privy filth and sin are what Harington has in mind when he claims to have attacked "pride and sensualitie."

The second section, according to this summary of the "true intent" of the book, is more personal: it "gives a due praise without flatterie, to one that is worthie of it, and a just checke without gall to some that deserve it." Donno identifies Essex as the individual Harington praises by comparison to "worthiest Trajan" (141). For the satire, Harington's obliquity has disguised individual topical references completely. Harington sums up the third section of the *New Discourse* thus: "as it teacheth indeed a reformation of the matter in question, so it toucheth in sport, a reprehension of some practises too much in custome." As we have seen, the practices satirized included the coy self-promotions of the inventor Hugh Plat and the iniquities of the monopoly system.

In a letter to Harington reporting the reaction at court to the *Metamorphosis*, Robert Markham says that the queen "did conceive much disquiet on being tolde you had aimed a shafte at Leicester: I wishe you knew the author of that ill deed. . . ."[19] This "shafte" has not been identified;[20] Leicester is referred to by name in the *Metamorphosis* in what seems to be neutral fashion (162). In any case the evidence in Harington's epigrams on the *Metamorphosis* suggests that the controversy it provoked was not a matter of satire on individuals but simply by virtue of its subject matter.[21]

Nashe himself was Harington's chief predecessor in the writing of what Harington calls "fantasticall Pamphlets." Nashe's technique involves self-consciousness about the act of writing, the dramatizing of his material, and exuberant wordplay. G. R. Hibbard says of him that "Instead of his eye being fixed on a topic, it is fixed on himself writing about that topic."[22]

Harington puts the new vehicle of the controversial pamphlet to different uses. Typically, Nashe's digressions enjoy equal status with the rest of his work: hierarchy is dispensed with and only one level is left, a succession of surfaces claiming equal attention. The relationship between medium and message is different in the *Metamorphosis:* in Donno's words, Harington, unlike Nashe, never allows his digressions "to over-shadow his essential concept of form and unity" (22). He is self-conscious about them: "But to step backe to my teshe (though every place I stept to, yeeldes mee sweeter discourse)" (101–2); "But now to the purpose, perhaps you will say, that this makes nothing to the present argument" (145). Nevertheless, they are true digressions, since the main thesis remains apparent beside them. References to rhetorical figures in the *Metamorphosis* indicate an allegiance to this mode of discourse: we hear of copiousness (86, 110), *reprehensio* (141), and *prolepsis* (208). In fact, many of Harington's terms suggest the model of a legal defense: he is "playing the lawyer" (120), and his references vary from quite general ones ("to defend by most autenticall authorities and examples, the use of these homely words in so necessary matters" [85]) to the technical ("al this while I have done litle better then confesse the action," that is, admit to the alleged fault [125]).

Harington's extravagances are generally metaphoric and paradoxical, rather than dramatic and descriptive, a discourse depending on allusions to classical learning and to the public and court affairs of his time. In the *New Discourse,* he quotes two Latin lines from the Oxford Protestant Dr. Laurence Humphrey comparing Elizabeth's purging of the English Church in the Reformation to the cleansing of the dung from the Augean stables. The context is a demonstration that homely terms have been used by the best authorities. Harington then reflects on the propriety of Humphrey's expression, and how best to render it in English:

. . . be it spoken without disgrace or dispraise to his poetrie, such a metaphor had bene fitter for a plaine Dame, abhorring all princely pompe,

and not refusing to weare russet [homespun] coates, then for the magnificent majestie of a Mayden Monark. Beleeve me, I would faine have
made him speake good rime in English, but (as I am a true μισακμοζ
[Misacmos]) I beate my braines about it, the space that one may go with
the tyde from London bridge, downe where the Priest fell in upon the
mayd, and from thence almost to Wapping, and yet I could not couch it
into a cleanly distichon. But yet because I know Mistress *Philostilpnos* will
have a great mind to know what it meanes, I will tell her by some handsome
circumlocution. His meaning is, that a Ladie of Ladies, did for zele to
the Lord of Lords, take the like pains to purge some Popish abuses, as
the great giantly Hercules did for Augeus. (105)

This passage of lively asides and miscellaneous academic foolery
exploits the persona of the writer, always before us as ironist of
himself, his authorities, and his subject; yet it never leaves for long
the main topic, the problem of making base facts "mannerly" and
its solution.

Harington must have learned something of the possibilities of
the controversial pamphlet from Nashe, in the use of the jester-
figure as highly visible spokesman, the value of kaleidoscopic variety
in keeping readers entertained, and the transformation of the relation
between writer and reader into dialogue or scene dramatically presented. Nevertheless, Nashe's prose moves toward liberating the
medium from its dedication to persuasion, while Harington's book
belongs better in the ambit of Humanist irony, turning the instru-
ments of rhetoric to unexpected purposes.

The Reformed Privy as Metaphor

Part of Harington's book takes the form of a treatise on obscenity,
a connected set of arguments aimed at redefining the concept and
making it serve a specific moral purpose. His discussion about
homely words and necessary matters in the early part of the *New
Discourse* turns on the idea that such words and such things are not
obscene in themselves, but are made so by the intent of the user
(83). In the Scriptures, for instance, there are phrases that seem
obscene,

and are so when they are used to ribauldrie, or lasciviousnesse, yet in the
Scripture they are not only void of incivilitie, but full of sanctitie; that
the Prophets do in no place more effectually, more earnestly, nor more

properly beate down our pride and vanitie, and open to our eyes the filthinesse, and horror of our sinnes, then by such kind of phrases. . . . (86)

Excrement, that is, can serve to remind man of his sinfulness, but the true obscenity is not in excrement but in sin.

Harington's treatise on obscenity constantly anticipates the charge that it is itself obscene. In rhetoric the anticipating of objections is called "prolepsis" or "procatalepsis." The figure is central to Harington's method in the *Metamorphosis*. For example, "Zoilus" and "Momus," who are pictured reading through the *New Discourse* at the beginning of the *Apologie,* first imagine it to be merely "scurrill, base, shallow, sordidous" stuff, and are well pleased. Then they are taken aback to discover that it has a satirical intent, and finding themselves named at the end of the "Prologue" sets them off "spitting & spalling, as though they had bene halfe choked" (208–9). Here the author himself depicts a reaction to his work, to make his satirical intentions unmistakable.

In a wider sense, the strategy of anticipating objections is the key to Harington's approach to obscenity in his book. He aims to provoke a scandalized reaction to one kind of scurrility—the modern term is lavatory humor—and then to contrast it with the truly dangerous obscenity of sin. A distinction is made between mere fastidiousness, an aversion from the "necessary matters" of natural bodily functions, and true virtue, which is aversion from sin. Shamed into disowning their reaction to the first, readers are prepared for the cloacinean satire's challenge to hypocrisy in invoking the second. Even Combe in the *Anatomie* touches on the point: "I smyle at some whose manners proove that thear mynds admit all wickednes, and yet forsooth theyr ears cannot brooke a litle scurrilytye" (200).

In the *New Discourse,* Harington illustrates his thesis on obscenity by a story he says his mother-in-law told his children.[23] A hermit was being conducted through a great city by an angel one evening to contemplate its wickedness. They first met a "gongfarmer" (dung carter) with a full cart; the hermit crosses the street, holding his nose, while the angel "kept on his way, seeming no whit offended with the savour." Not long after, a woman passes by "gorgeously attyred, well perfumed, well attended with coaches, and torches," a courtesan on her way to an assignation. The hermit, "somewhat revived with the faire sight, and sweet savour," stops to stare; now it is the angel's turn to hold his nose and hurry away. The hermit

more marvelling than before, he was told by the Angell, that this fine
courtesan laden with sinne, was a more stinking savour afore God & his
holy Angels, then that beastly cart, laden with excrements. (85)

The moral is that the truly dangerous sinners are those who deny
the animal side of humanity and disguise it with finery.

It was Luther who associated Satan and evil most forcefully with
dung, creating in Norman O. Brown's words "a grossly concrete
image of the anal character of the Devil."[24] One of Satan's wiles,
he thought, was to shame man into admitting the obscenity of his
bodily part. Harington has an illustrated epigram in his *Metamorphosis* giving an answer to this stratagem (Luther had told the same
story[25]). "A godly father," sitting on the privy, mumbled certain
prayers.

> . . . unto him the Devil straight repayr's:
> And boldly to revile him he begins,
> Alledging that such prayr's are deadly sins;
> And that it shewd, he was devoyd of grace,
> To speake to God, from so unmeete a place.

The godly father is dismayed at first, but his faith is strong, and
he retorts,

> To God my pray'r I meant, to thee the durt.
> Pure prayr ascends to him that high doth sit,
> Down fals the filth, for fiends of hel more fit.
>   (94)

The reformed jakes is the basis of the underlying conceit of the
book, the comparison between dung and sin, and the contrast between fastidiousness and true virtue. As T. G. A. Nelson points
out, it is "the parallel between the need to reform the evil-smelling
privies in men's houses and the need to amend the sordid vices in
their lives" that unites the various parts of the *Metamorphosis*.[26] On
one hand, the parallel may show the difficulty of reforming souls:

I will wish all the readers may find as sure a way to cleanse, and keepe
sweete the noblest part of them selves, that is, their soules; as I shall shew
them a plaine and easie way, to keep sweet the basest part of their houses,
that is, their sinkes [sewers]. (85)

Or, on the other hand, in the spirit of the angel and the hermit, it may serve to show the offensiveness of sin:

Beleeve it (worthie readers, for I write not to the unworthie) A Jax when he is at his worst, yeelds not a more offensive savour to the finest nosthrils, then some of the faults I have noted do, to God and the world. (183)

The Mock Encomium

In exploiting a subject outside polite discourse for inversions of values, Harington was writing in the tradition of the mock encomium. Other men, he says in his letter in the *New Discourse,* "with great prayse of wit, though small of modestie, have written of worse matters." His list of mock encomiums begins with Erasmus's *Praise of Folly* and ends with "a beastly treatise onely to examine what is the fittest thing to wype withall"—by Rabelais, as his footnote points out (63–64 and n. c).

The mock encomium applied the forms of the encomium, the treatise of praise, to unworthy subjects like insomnia, to unpopular characters like Thersites, and to base natural facts like dust and dung. As Arthur Stanley Pease observes, it was "freer in its arrangement than the more strictly logical forms of eloquence," and "laid chief emphasis upon the number, variety, and unexpected character of the arguments adduced for praise."[27] It was an opportunity for a display of virtuosity, reversing the expected and exploiting paradox. Lucian in the *The Parasite,* for instance, parodies defenses of legitimate arts by proving "That Sponging is a Profession." In the late Renaissance, according to Pease, mock encomiums tended to stress the satiric rather than the rhetorical element.[28]

The form was an ideal vehicle for Humanist irony. *The Praise of Folly* is especially complex because Folly is the author as well as the subject of her encomium: everything she says in her oration is foolish by virtue of its speaker. It also becomes clear that there may be some truth in her assertions that there is an element of folly, of unworldly innocence and ecstasy, in true religious feeling: she points to the way children, old people, and the retarded are delighted with the Mass; to the way those who give themselves up to religion abandon all common sense, "throw away their possessions, ignore injuries, allow themselves to be deceived, make no distinction between friend and foe, shudder at the thought of pleasure, find satisfaction in fasts, vigils, tears, and labors." It is no wonder, she says, that the apostles seemed to be drunk on new wine, and the judge Festus thought Paul was mad.[29]

Transmutations of a similar kind take place in Panurge's praise of debt in Rabelais: borrowing and lending become the essential foundation for all charity, and thus for the interdependence of humanity. In a world without lending, Panurge says, people will not even greet one another,

it will be but lost labour to expect aid or succour from any, or to cry fire, water, murder, for none will put to their helping hand. Why? He lent no money, there is nothing lent to him . . . In short, Faith, Hope, and Charity would be quite banished from such a world,—for men are born to relieve and assist one another . . .[30]

The mixture of humor and seriousness and the oblique irony in these two exercises in the mock encomium required a sophisticated interpretation from their readers. Erasmus had to defend himself against those who took Folly's statements at face value and accused him of impiety.[31] Rabelais was also aware of the vicissitudes of interpretation that an ironic work of this kind must undergo. In his prologue to *Gargantua* he quotes Plato's conceit of the Sileni, boxes painted outside with grotesque figures and ludicrously deformed and fantastical animals yet containing things of great value inside: balms, perfumes, and precious stones. Rabelais says his book is like the Sileni. Though a cursory reading of its titles and headings may suggest only "jests, mockeries, lascivious discourse, and recreative lies," yet serious consideration will show "that it containeth things of far higher value than the box did promise; that is to say, that the subject thereof is not so foolish, as by the title at first sight it would appear to be."

Rabelais then gives a second analogy for the doubleness of his book, and the way the reader should approach it: like a dog with a bone, he must "by a sedulous lecture, and frequent meditation, break the bone, and suck out the marrow; that is, my allegorical sense," a profound and abstruse doctrine in matters of religion and "the public state and life economical."[32]

The Sileni and the bone and the marrow formulate neatly the relationship between the literal and ironic meanings of these texts. *The Metamorphosis of Ajax* belongs with them, treating as it does an indecorous subject with elaborate jesting, and turning its grotesque form inside out to disarm hypocrisy and reorder values. Rabelais's prologue provides a gloss for Robert Markham's tantalizing comment on the reception of Harington's work at court in 1598: "Your book is almoste forgiven, and I may say forgotten; but not for its lacke of wit or satyr . . . tho' her Highnesse signified displeasure in outwarde sorte, yet did she like the marrowe of your booke."[33]

Harington quotes Rabelais, and seems from manuscript evidence to have had a copy of his works beside him when he revised his draft.[34] Rabelais and Erasmus are sources for the matrix of Humanist irony it uses, and "Rabelaisian" has been a common epithet for the *Metamorphosis*. Huntington Brown puts Harington among the first English Rabelaisians, capturing "the charm of his miscellaneous learning, his mock-gravity, and his healthy coarseness."[35] Jack Lindsay described the *Metamorphosis* as a "nonsensical bombination" leading to an explication of one of the base facts of life, and a Rabelaisian "paean to a life which happens to include such homely facts and the possibility of such nonsense."[36]

Yet Harington's outlook is different from that of Rabelais. The latter's Silenus box has a grotesque, blatantly scurrilous outside, and a humane, liberal message ("Do What Thou Wilt") inside. As M. A. Screech points out, Rabelais can make the body and its works funny because he has faith in the divine part of man, his mind, and in the principle that natural things cannot be base, *naturalia non sunt turpia*.[37] This faith in nature, and human nature in particular, gives buoyancy to the torrents of gross physicality in Rabelais: torrents like the floods of Gargantua's urine that sweep away the last bastions of prudery and even of proverbial common sense.

Harington's Silenus, on the other hand, has an air of learnedly witty obscenity outside and a tolerant but admonitory reminder within. He draws a stern parallel between the reformation of the privy—which is practicable—and the daunting task of reforming souls. For Harington, sin is a reality, and excretion a reminder of it—a reminder (as we have seen) of the fleshly corruption even the proudest and most sanctimonious share.

The *Metamorphosis* exploits obscenity where Rabelais abolishes the very notion: Harington operates by innuendo and insinuation, and at, rather than beyond, a barrier between polite discourse and scurrility. His invention aims to civilize the privy, and his argument is that the privy as a subject should be brought within the ambit of civilized discourse. He has himself made it mannerly, has clothed

it "like an ape in purple" (65).[38] One of his implied arguments is
that if the privy cannot even be discussed, because it is too base to
be treated seriously, then it will continue to be a noisome thing.
His book itself is intended as an example of the civilized treatment
of a scurrilous subject, a parallel to the reformed "forme" of his
privy, which makes tolerable its malodorous "matter."

Nevertheless, Harington follows Rabelais in a prose that is a
reckless squandering of words, a fit antidote for the fastidious hyp-
ocrites whose pedantic treatises and squeamish manners are his implicit targets. In Combe's word, his subject is not so much clarified
as "eliquidated." Rabelais was clearly the model for the style of
some of the liveliest parts of the *Metamorphosis,* and contributed to
its richly allusive fantasy and giddyingly nimble syntax. Huntington
Brown found a passage in it "exactly in the manner of Rabelais's
prologues"; [39] in the *New Discourse* Rabelais's hero Gargantua actually
appears: having mowed the grass that was sacred to Ajax to use in
his privy, he was "stricken in his Posteriorums with S. Anthonies
fier," went on a pilgrimage, and on his return vowed

that of all offices of the house, he should do honour to that house of office,
where he had committed that scorne to AJAX: and that there, he should
never use any more such fine grasse, but rather, teare a leafe out of
Holinsheds *Chronicles,* or some of the books that lye in the hall; then to
commit such a sinne against AJAX. Wherefore immediatly on his comming
home, he built a sumptuous privie, and in the most conspicuous place
thereof, namely just over the doore; he erected a statue of AJAX, with so
grim a countenance, that the aspect of it being full of terrour, was halfe
as good as a suppositor; and further, to honour him he chaunged the name
of the house, and called it after the name of this noble Captaine of the
greasie ones (the Grecians I should say) AJAX: though since, by ill pronunciation, and by a figure called *Cacophonia,* the accent is changed and
it is called a Jakes. (68–71)

Conclusion

Harington's book is constructed out of a matrix of doubleness,
on the model of the Silenus or the bone-and-marrow of Humanist
irony. It calls itself at various times a pill in an apple, wormwood
in raisins, an ape in purple, a fair face behind a grotesque mask.
Its author admits to being a jester with a serious tale to tell. Even
the marrow within the bone is double: part the reformation of the

privy, part the reformation of souls. Not surprisingly, interpretation of the *Metamorphosis* was problematic from the beginning. Immediate reactions like Nashe's in his letter and Misodiaboles' in *Ulysses upon Ajax* suggested puzzlement and a sense that Harington had blundered. Nashe literalizes the book about privies into a malodorous object, a stool wrapped in paper; the play of distinctions in the *Metamorphosis* between excrement and obscenity, between filth filthily treated and filth discussed in a civilized way, between the old stinking jakes and the reformed one, went for nothing. As late as 1611, Hugh Holland was reproached for associating himself with Harington and abandoning the Muses for dedication to Stercutius, the god of dung, and to "strong-smelling facetiousnesses" like the *Metamorphosis*.[40]

Ulysses upon Ajax finds satirical ammunition in the idea that Harington has been disastrously indiscreet in applying his admittedly nimble wit on an obscene subject: wit and folly have been fatally yoked in the *Metamorphosis*, overturning the chariot of reason. For Misodiaboles the indecency is especially appalling in one of Harington's mature years, noble birth, solid fortune, and powerful connections.[41] At court a Star Chamber suit threatened, and though the queen liked the "marrow" of the book, its wit and satire, she did not wish to see the author at court again "till he hath grown sober, and leaveth the ladies sportes and frolicks."[42]

The *Metamorphosis* did find an honorable place in the tradition of the mock encomium, however, and was soon to appear alongside other well-known examples like *The Praise of Folly* and Synesius's encomium on baldness.[43] Even Nashe seems to have changed his mind about it: his list of the writers of mock encomiums in *Nashes Lenten Stuffe* (1599) includes Harington, as one who "offers sacrifice to the goddesse *Cloaca*, and disportes himselfe very schollerly and wittilie about the reformation of close stooles and houses of office, and spicing and embalming their rancke intrails, that they stincke not."[44] John Taylor gave a flattering view of the reception of Harington's book in *The Praise of Hemp-seed* (1620):

> A learned Knight, of much esteeme and worth,
> A pamphlet of a privy did set forth,
> Which strong breath'd Ajax was well lik'd, because
> Twas writ with wit and did deserve applause.[45]

The pun on "Ajax" and "a jakes" did not originate with Harington's book. It appears in *Love's Labour's Lost,* written about 1594 (in act 5, scene 2). Nevertheless, the frequency of allusions to the pun after 1596 seems to be at least partly a tribute to the popularity of the *Metamorphosis.* John Marston talks of a rhyme that "stincks like Ajax froth" in 1598;[46] "Ajax" is used as a synonym for "privy" in epigrams, translations, and verses well into the seventeenth century.[47] Touchstone calls Jacques "Master What-ye-call't" in *As You Like It* (3.3.66), perhaps as a tribute to the topicality of the slang title "jakes" for the privy.[48] Harington's essay in the facetiously erudite treatment of homely subjects inspired his readers to a variety of conceits; Donne, for instance, included an imaginary volume by Harington called *Hercules, or the method of purging Noah's Ark of excrement* in his mock catalog of books, *Catalogus Librorum Aulicorum.*[49] Harington himself became known as "Sir Ajax." Truewit, in Jonson's *Epicoene* (1609), suggests to La Fool that "A stool were better, sir, of Sir Ajax his invention."[50]

Harington got himself talked about, as he meant to, by publishing the *Metamorphosis;* but in his own time, and since, it was notoriety rather than advancement or admiration that he achieved. His literary reputation has never quite rid itself of the taint of the privy. As he feared, his *prolepses* were ignored and his book was "taken at the volley" (216). Schelling's remark in his preface to the *Epigrams and Letters* edition of 1930 may stand for the prevailing attitude in the years before Donno's edition of the *Metamorphosis* in 1962:

he set forth his argument in terms so ingeniously gross, if at times so perversely learned, that he has deserved the consequent neglect, if not altogether the obloquy, into which his name has fallen. With *The Metamorphosis of Ajax* we have happily nothing to do.[51]

The present-day reader, who may be freer than Schelling was to accept Harington's insistence that his treatise on obscenity was not itself obscene, and in a post-Freudian era less hasty in dismissing any treatment of Harington's subject, still faces insuperable obstacles to a satisfactory interpretation. To recover the proper context for the *Metamorphosis* now requires an effort of historical reconstruction, yet any solemnly academic treatment of Harington's parody of a scholarly treatise may miss the point, or itself risk ludicrousness. In any case, Harington chose to be highly topical, and to be oblique in doing so: the result is that most of the allusions to contemporary events and personalities in the *Metamorphosis* are lost for good. Donno's edition, with over 330 footnotes, is a valiant attempt to reconstruct the learning and gossip at the fingertips of the courtly reader of 1596, but even she confesses not infrequently to bafflement.

We are left with a text that remains a specimen of exuberantly lively prose and a complex example of the mock encomium. "Misodiaboles" warned that for the chariot of *The Metamorphosis of Ajax* wit and folly had been recklessly yoked together. At least we can see better than he could that the combination is essential to Harington's scheme and to his twin aims of entertaining his reader and challenging hypocrisy in his society.

Chapter Four
The Epigrams

Predecessors and Sources

Between about 1589 and 1603, Harington wrote over 430 epigrams. Only one (in a Latin translation) was published in his lifetime,[1] yet he was soon established among the leading English exponents of the genre. Charles Fitz-Geffrey, for instance, puts Harington ahead of John Heywood and Sir John Davies as English epigrammatists in a poem published in 1601.[2] Certainly, Harington's verses were avidly collected, especially at court and at the Inns of Court. In his *Index of English Literary Manuscripts,* Peter Beal lists thirty-seven seventeenth-century manuscript versions of one of the epigrams, and twenty-five of another.[3]

Harington was one of the pioneers in a revival of the epigram form in Elizabethan times. The epigram became a vehicle for the satirical vogue of the 1590s, being, as Edward Guilpin puts it in *Skialethia* (1598), "a plaine dealing lad, that is not afraid / To speake the truth, but calls a jade, a jade." On the other hand, a distinction was made between epigrams and the more trenchant forms of verse satire, modeled on the works of Juvenal and christened by Guilpin "the scourge, the *Tamberlaine* of vice."[4]

The epigrammatists and satirists of the 1590s rejected what they saw as the debased Petrarchanism of the poetry of their day, and even the vogue for romance to which Harington's *Orlando* belonged. They claimed they were replacing the hackneyed and saccharine insipidity of the sonnet and the foolish fantasies of the romance with a tough realism. Joseph Hall, who called himself the first of the English satirists, scorned tales like those in *Orlando* as fit only to "rocke asleep our drouzy Syres." Guilpin rejected what he called "whimpring Sonnets, puling Elegies," in favor of satire.[5] Harington puts the contrast between sonnet and epigram in terms of sugar and salt in Epigram no. 38. "Faustus" prefers the sonnet:

Their sugred taste best likes his likresse [dainty] senses.
Well, though I grant Sugar may please the taste,
Yet let my verse have salt to make it last.

The word *epigram* derives from the Greek word for inscription, and the form seems to have originated in commemorative notices on monuments and tombs. Certainly the brevity of inscriptions, and their public nature, have always been associated with the epigram.[6] A contemporary of Harington's, George Puttenham, even suggests that epigrams developed from classical *graffiti:*

this *Epigramme* is but an inscription or writting made as it were upon a table, or in a windowe, or upon the wall or mantell of a chimney in some place of common resort . . . as now in our tavernes and common tabling houses, where many merry heads meete, and scrible with ynke with chalke, or with a cole such matters as they would every man should know, & descant upon.[7]

The Renaissance inherited two different traditions of the epigram. The earlier of the two is represented by the Greek Anthology, which consists of epigrams from early classical to medieval times preserved in two Byzantine collections, known as the Palatine and the Planudean Anthologies. The editor of a modern edition defines the epigram of the Greek Anthology as a very short poem "summing up as though in a memorial inscription what it is desired to make permanently memorable in a single action or situation. It must have the compression and conciseness of a real inscription, and in proportion to the smallness of its bulk must be highly finished, evenly balanced, simple, and lucid."[8]

The other epigram tradition is the creation of the Roman poet Martial (A.D. ca. 40–ca. 104). Where the epigrams in the Anthology are evocative, elegiac, amatory or convivial, Martial's are personal, colloquial, urban, and satiric. Martial's laconic realism, his sharp eye for detail, and his cynical attitudes created the form that we now think of as characteristically "epigrammatic."[9]

It was Martial's example that was the more influential for Harington and for the revival of the epigram in the 1590s. Martial presents epigrams as entertaining trifles, to be enjoyed when the serious business of the day is over. At the end of one epigram, Martial warns his book not to give a drunken knock at Pliny's door in the daytime:

seras tutior ibis ad lucernas:
haec hora est tua, cum furit Lyaeus,
cum regnat rosa, cum madent capilli:
tunc me vel rigidi legant Catones.

(Safer will you go at the time of the late-kindled lamps; that hour is yours
when Lyaeus is in revel, when the rose is queen, when locks are drenched.
Then let even unbending Catos read me.) (10.19)[10]

Along with this attitude goes a certain scorn for the pomposities
and extravagant inventions of epic and tragic literature. There are
no Centaurs or Harpies in his pages, Martial says: his subject is
man (10.4). Martial's realism generally has a satiric bent, and he
is obliged to assure his audience that his target is not any one person,
but the social abuse itself: "hunc servare modum nostri novere li-
belli, / parcere personis, dicere de vitiis" ("This measure my books
learn to keep, to spare the person, to denounce the vice" [10.33]).
He also feels obliged to defend himself for the lasciviousness of his
epigrams, blaming it on the demands of popular taste (1.35). In
any case, he says, "lasciva est nobis pagina, vita proba" ("wanton
is my page; my life is good" [1.4]).

One last feature of Martial's work that finds an echo in his six-
teenth- and seventeenth-century followers in England is its depiction
of an active, self-conscious literary milieu: the epigrams address a
critical audience that must be satisifed and, on occasions, instructed
in how to appreciate Martial's verses; at times his readers must even
be rebuked for plagiarizing his work by reciting or writing it as if
it were their own. Epigrams are glimpsed circulating, criticizing
one another, defending themselves, and borrowing with or without
acknowledgment from one another, in a tissue of references to a
sophisticated urban culture.

McClure's edition listed fifty-four of Harington's epigrams as
having a source in Martial; Jean Humez increased the number to
over eighty.[11] Harington cheerfully acknowledges his borrowings.
He mentions in no. 388 that he and Sir John (then Mr. John) Davies
have been accused of stealing "good conceits from Martiall," but
replies that Surrey, Wyatt and Heywood did the same: if they are
thieves, they are in honorable company. The relationship of epigram
to original in Harington's collection covers a wide spectrum. Sometimes an imitation is announced as such by a title mentioning that

it is "out of *Martial*" (e.g., no. 144), or by opening lines beginning "In Rome . . ." (no. 171). In no. 255, by contrast, Harington achieves true translation: he preserves the pointedness of the original, while the result seems authentically part of his own world. Martial has: "Quem recitas meus est, O Fidentine, libellus: / sed male cum recitas, incipit esse tuus" ("That book you recite, O Fidentinus, is mine. But your vile recitation begins to make it your own" [1.38]). Harington's version is "To an ill Reader" (no. 255): "The verses, *Sextus,* thou doost read, are mine; / But with bad reading thou wilt make them thine." More commonly, details or arguments are added to Martial's outline to make it more explicit. Sometimes the changes adapt the original to new purposes, as when a dwarf becomes a puppy (no. 283, following Martial, 12.93), or the focus of the poem becomes a young girl instead of a mistress (no. 76, following Martial 11.27).

Generally, Harington fills out Martial's elliptical style into something altogether more robust. Martial 1.73 is about Caecilianus's prostituting of his wife:

> Nullus in urbe fuit tota qui tangere vellet
>   uxorem gratis, Caeciliane, tuam,
> dum licuit: sed nunc positis custodibus ingens
>   turba fututorum est. ingeniosus homo es.

(There was no one in the whole town willing to touch your wife, Caecilianus, gratis, while he was allowed; but, now you have set your guards, there is a huge crowd of pokers. You are an ingenious person!)

Harington follows in no. 96:

> *Cayus,* none reckned of thy wife a poynt,
> While each might, without all let or cumber,
> But since a watch o're her thou didst appoint,
> Of Customers she hath no little number.
>   Well, let them laugh hereat that list, and scoffe it,
>   But thou do'st find what makes most for thy profit.

Martial makes his point in a sly, laconic statement in the second half of his last line. Harington makes his in an emphatic and explicit couplet, with a heavy rhyme. The poise of Martial's epigram is in its elegant asymmetry, a conclusion shorter than expected, which turns the reader from scorning Caecilianus to acknowledging his cunning. Harington's Caius has his revenge on his mockers when his motives are spelled out. The result is solidly symmetrical. Martial's nimble verses crystallize an attitude or an exchange in a few lines, closing on a deft side-step; Harington's rely on a heavier emphasis and rhythm and solid touches of local color.

Harington only rarely matches the barbed urbanity of his model. All the same, Martial provided a sardonic view of the world that could be made to fit Harington's own experience with remarkable closeness. No. 147, "To My Lady *Rogers,*" tells how he sent Lady Rogers a cask of claret and a stag, when she made his wife her heir. All the neighbors feasted off them, but Harington was not invited; he hopes his wife's promised inheritance is safe, "Else, I might doubt I should your Land inherit, / That of my stagge did not one morsell merit." The epigram seems to come directly from Harington's own experience, located in a specific time and place and in his feelings of righteous indignation ("Each man I meet hath filled up his panch"). Yet there is a direct model in Martial 9.48, where the poet has sent Garricus a boar on the strength of his hopes for a quarter of Garricus's estate, yet has had no part of the feast that follows, while "ructat adhuc aprum pallida Roma meum" ("a bilious Rome is still belching my boar"): "de quadrante tuo quid sperem, Garrice? nulla / de nostro nobis uncia venit apro" ("Concerning that quarter-estate of yours, what should I expect, Garricus? Not a twelfth of my own boar came to me!"). Harington's experience fits neatly into the form the Roman original provides, a complex attitude combining reproach for the target of the epigram and self-ridicule in the speaker, whose hopes are so humiliatingly clouded while all and sundry enjoy his largesse.

Harington has a few pages on epigrams in *The Metamorphosis of Ajax,* discussing writers in the form he knew and admired. "It is certaine," he says, "that of all poems, the Epigram is the plesawntest, & of all that writes Epigrams, Martial is counted the wittyest" (97). He goes on to give samples from Sir Thomas More's Latin epigrams "that flie over all Europe for their wit and conceit" (99–100). One of the jester-figures quoted is John Heywood, who "for his Proverbs & Epigrams, is not yet put downe by any of our countrey" (102–3). Nearest him in achievement is Harington's contemporary Sir John Davies, here obliquely referred to.

More and Heywood (after Martial) are thus Harington's models. More's epigrams, first published in 1518, borrow from the Planudean Anthology, rather than from Martial, but More does emphasize the witty and satiric possibilities of the form. More's collection also reflects a northern European tradition of folk wisdom: one epigram is entitled, "A Laughable Tale about the King and the Dutch Peasant"; another warns that "If you let your wife stamp on your foot tonight, tomorrow she will rise early to stamp on your head."[12]

John Heywood's epigrams (first published in full in 1562) are almost entirely in this vein: narrative and sententious, constructed around the unfolding of a story, or the expansion of a proverb, not (as in Martial) around the turn of a conclusion. There are no proper names but only stock figures identified as "A big breecht man" or the like; often, the epigram takes the impersonal, general form of a proverb. The setting is mainly rural, populated by rats, wrens, hares, dogs, and fleas. Heywood is no railing satirist or cynic: in his *Epigrams* he calls himself "Heywood with the mad mery wit."[13]

There are a number of epigrams about Heywood in Harington's collection, based on his writings (nos. 30, 326, 388) or on stories about his life (nos. 182, 198, 199). A number of Harington's proverbial sayings occur also in Heywood: the catchphrase "love me, love my dog" from no. 72, "To his Wife for striking her Dogge," is also in Heywood's *A Dialogue Containing Proverbs;* the proverbial saying "as fierce as a Cotswold lion [i.e., as a sheep]" is used in no. 216 and in Heywood.[14] Heywood's stance as a popular philosopher, drawing on accumulated common experience preserved in traditional tales and sayings, is an important source for the characteristic mode of Harington's epigrams.

Harington's Instructions to the Reader

Harington's "Epistle to all," introducing the epigrams, appeals for an attentive reading. These poems, he says, are not to be attacked greedily like the first or the second course of a meal, but, like the fruit, nuts, cheese, and raisins of dessert, they should be sampled a few at a time:

> So shall you finde some coole, some warme, some biting,
> Some sweet in taste, some sharpe, all so delighting,
> As may your inward taste, and fancie tickle.
>
> (no. 1)

Harington's epigrams, then, are not presented as the substantial fare of literature, but as miscellaneous trifles. Elsewhere in the collection he calls them "the fruitlesse fruits of idle houres" (no. 200). Harington is an amateur; his Muse

> . . . never sought to set to sale her wryting;
> In part her friends, in all her selfe delighting,
> She cannot beg applause of vulgar sort,
> Free born and bred, more free for noble sport.

A voice tells her, "Yf well disposed, to write; yf not, forbear" (no. 424). The nonchalance of the amateur epigrammatist is a contrast to the commercialization of sonnet-writing: professional poets, as no. 41 tells us, need no longer be poor because there is now a trade in sonnets; Don Pedro, according to no. 40, bought the verses he touts as his own for two crowns each. The amateur can afford to be honest: while others' Muses "fayn," Harington will concern himself with "trew discourse" (no. 424). Feigning is associated with flattery and self-advertisement, and Harington's epigrams will not stoop to these, however much this may displease the reader who does not enjoy hearing the truth (no. 60).

Yet Harington does not want to abandon the idea that there is a useful and a serious side to his epigrams. In no. 160 he urges the epigrammatist and minister Thomas Bastard not to stop writing because the envious have scoffed at his efforts. While the preacher in the pulpit must treat of "matters serious," and "high things mysterious," elsewhere there must be room for "honest sports," which refresh us, spur us on, when wholesome things leave us sated and dull. Moreover, Bastard's verses are intended to improve men's manners, and any such reminder of our sinfulness is useful. These are casually inclusive arguments in favor of the epigram: they suggest that Harington was aiming at toleration for their existence rather than arguing in any spirit of earnest partisanship. He is skeptical, in any case, about how much can be learned from books: in no. 3 he says, "Bookes give not wisedome where was none before. / But where some is, there reading makes it more."

Harington is nonchalant about the weight and worth of his epigrams, but where they are challenged he is prepared to defend them, if unsystematically, on the grounds that they perform a useful function in society. Similarly, for all his casualness, he will not let the accusation that his epigrams are carelessly written go by without a retort. They may seem simple and unlabored, but just as a smoothly fitting bodice takes more work than an ill-fitting one, so the work of "Writers wits, / Was hardest wrought, when as it smoothest sits" (no. 208). Harington makes only modest claims for his verses, but he does not wish his readers to read hastily through them, or mistake their casual air for carelessness. The epigrammatist may be after all most like a confectioner, but there is pleasure and some nourishment to be had from him and he wishes his workmanship to be appreciated.

To "Mix Serious Things with Jests"

It seems, then, that Harington does not resolve the relationship between the pleasure and the usefulness of the epigram in any systematic way—does not present any theory of poetry, that is— but adopts a strategy of first conceding mere pleasurableness and then (almost paradoxically) asserting that there will always be some good use to be made of the epigram. This casualness reflects his suspicion of rigid systems in the moral sphere, and his tolerant view of lapses from them. To be aware of man's sinfulness is to doubt puritanical strictures on behavior and to take pleasure in human nature showing itself incompatible with inflexible rules. Not only is pleasure good in itself, but man's need for it is also a reminder of the demands of human nature and thus ultimately of man's sinfulness. Ideally, then, the humor of the epigram can be at the same time satire (an awareness of the ludicrous gap between human nature and human pretensions), pleasure (a relief from the demands of higher forms of literature, and broadly, from work and duty), and instruction (as a touchstone of the frailty of human nature, encouraging humility and dissolving hypocrisy).

Books, and the epigram least of all, cannot reform the reader, but they can remind him of his sinfulness. Even a book proving that shoemaking is a noble craft should not be scorned: after all, its value would be unmatched

> If so with Gentle Craft it could perswade
> Great Princes midst their pompe to learne a trade,
> Once in their lives to worke, to mend their soules.
>   (no. 265)

The epigram is about the way books can be turned to moral purposes, but it is also an instance in miniature of such an act: the wordplay is a reminder of final things carried in a pleasurable conceit.

The epigrammatic mode itself fits this mixture of tolerance and seriousness exactly. Unpretentious, occasional, aiming mainly to amuse, it deflates pomposity and exposes hypocrisy by placing them beside its own good humor, a genial recognition of human weakness that is also a knowledge of the vanity of things in the fallen world. As Humez points out, it is the "sweet sinne" of lust that serves Harington most often as a particular touchstone.[15] Of the sins, he finds lechery the easiest to forgive, "a lively not a deadly sinn" (no. 408); he admits his love for his wife is bound up with lust (no. 390). The Puritan members of no. 356 are "of the weakest sex and purest sect"; no. 413 brings puritanism and a sexual lapse still closer together in its title, "Of a pregnant pure sister." A "Cloystered Frier" in no. 339, sworn to rigid Counter-Reformation chastity, is troubled with a priapism, which can only be cured in a brothel. After the treatment, he makes loud lamentation, not for his sin but because he has lived so long without it. The humor of the epigram springs from the flesh asserting itself against the spirit.

The epigrams attacking the marriage of the clergy are a good instance of Harington's particular mode of mixing "wisely . . . serious things with Jests," in his own phrase (no. 419). He says in 1607 that he had the queen very much in mind as an audience in these epigrams—knowing her dislike for such marriages made him all the bolder in glancing "somwhat unhappily, but rather plesantly than maliciously against preists marriages."[16] His theme is essentially that such marriages make priests worldly, make them wallow in "flesh and bloud"; here, it seems, bodily weakness is not to be allowed to suborn the spirit. He finds it difficult to think of the children of priests as legitimate, which, in the case of Thomas Bastard, is at least appropriate (no. 358). No. 359 develops a comparison between the priests of old, who used to build for the Church, and the new clergy, who put all their energy into producing children:

> Was that a pryde in preests, or was yt piety?
> Had those more zeall, or wer they more presumptuos
> To build soch Colledges for their society,

With abbyes well endowd and Churches sumptuos?
If that wear pride, have ours too much humility?
If theirs wear zeall, have ours no godly mocion?
Yes! I can proove that ours both have abillity,
And that they build much more with more devocion.
With stone, yea, with free stones, they rear of building,
Worlds pretty, mycrocosmous, little ones,
With temples tymbred well, and som have guilding.
Shrines not of dead men's but of lively bones;
Thease buildings walk, oh! works worth admyracion,
And each beares sirname of their archytector.
And as yt ought Love layd the first foundacion,
But Love read in St. Luke with Ovids lector.
    Well, sith this building from those old one varyes,
    Som men could wish such builders had no quaryes.

A serious unease with what Harington sees as corruption in the institution of the Church is expressed here, in the epigram's ironic praise of the clergy's new sort of building.

Harington's interest in mixing entertainment and serious purpose in his epigrams is reflected in his admiration for those who used their jests to turn the wrath of their sovereign or to instruct this all-powerful person without lèse-majesté. In a passage in the *Metamorphosis* on Sir Thomas More already cited, Harington describes More's jests on the eve of his execution. One involved his negotiations with the king over the oath of supremacy, which made the king supreme head of the Church in England, and which he had formerly refused to sign. When asked if he had changed his mind, he answered, yes, but when the king's man came to collect his signature,

Oh sayd he, I have not changed my mind in that matter, but onely in this; I thought to have sent for a Barber, to have bene shaven ere I had died, but now if it please the King, he shal cut off head, and beard, and all together. (101)

As we have seen, Harington risked a jest himself when confronted with Elizabeth's fury after the debacle of Essex's expedition to Ireland. Threatened with the Fleet prison, he "answered poetically, 'that coming so late from the land-service, I hoped that I should not be prest to serve her Majesty's fleet in Fleet-street.' " In one of the epigrams, he tells how John Heywood visited Queen Mary on her deathbed; she complained that her doctors' cure was to make her sweat, a treatment so painful that she would rather die. Heywood, fearing what would happen to Catholics like himself if her Protestant half-sister Elizabeth should succeed her, replied "with cheerefull face, but cheerelesse soule,"

> Sweet Lady, you must sweat, or else, I swear it,
> We shall all sweat for it, if you forbeare it.
>   (no. 182)

Harington himself has some epigrams on delicate matters of state. No. 336 is titled "A Tragicall Epigram":

> When doome of Peeres & Judges fore-appointed,
> By racking lawes beyond all reach of reason,
> Had unto death condemn'd a Queene anointed,
> And found, (oh strange!) without allegeance, treason,
> The Axe that should have done that execution,
> Shunn'd to cut off a head that had been crowned,
> Our hangman lost his wonted resolution,
> To quell a Queene of nobles so renowned.
> Ah, is remorse in hangmen and in steele,
> Where Peeres and Judges no remorse can feele?
>   Grant Lord, that in this noble Ile, a Queene
>   Without a head, may never more be seene.

The verse is hurried forward by the indignant alliterations ("beyond all reach of reason," "To quell a Queene") to the question that brings the reluctant axe and executioner at Mary Queen of Scots' execution together with the merciless peers and judges of the opening lines: "Ah, is remorse in hangmen and in steele, / When Peeres and Judges no remorse can feele?" The couplet that follows takes up the idea of beheading but diverges perceptibly. This throws a special emphasis on the "Queene / Without a head." As Humez has shown, the ordering of the Folger presentation manuscript indicates that this is a play on words. Immediately preceding no. 336 in the Folger sequence is an epigram "Of Treason" (no. 259):

> Treason doth never prosper, what's the reason?
> For if it prosper, none dare call it Treason.

More importantly, the epigram before that is no. 189, "Of Monsters.
To my Lady *Rogers*." All sorts of "Strange-headed Monsters" are
described, but the epigram ends by declaring that "A headlesse
woman is a greater Monster" than any of them. Here the "headless
woman" is a woman without a husband, like the widow Lady Rogers.
It is clear that by the "Queene / Without a head" of two epigrams
later is meant the unmarried Queen Elizabeth as well as the queen
who is the victim of her mercilessness.[17] The obliquity of Harington's treatment of this dangerous question protects him: even in its
sequence, the play on words is a supposition and could be safely
denied by its creator. Harington has chosen to mix serious things
and jests "wisely" here, rather than in the spirit of the "apothegms"
More coined in the face of death itself.

Formal Qualities

Lessing defined the epigram by its two-part form, *Erwartung* or
expectation followed by *Aufschluss* or conclusion.[18] In the simplest
of Harington's epigrams, the steps have a line each:

> *Don Pedro's* out of debt, be bold to say it,
> For they are said to owe, that meane to pay it. (no. 65)

The intensive "be bold to say it" suggests that the statement "*Don
Pedro's* out of debt" is a daring one. The expectation thus awakened
is satisfied by an especially narrow definition of "to owe"—that
those who do not intend to pay do not truly "owe," and thus no
longer think of themselves as debtors. This epigram, like the more
famous "Of Treason" already quoted, is short enough to have been
passed around as court gossip; the form preserves the tiny gesture
of wit and the flick of its worldly, cynical mockery.

The laconic epigram is the exception rather than the rule in
Harington's collection. More typical is no. 142, "A pretty questions
[*sic*] of *Lazarus* soule well answered":

> Once on occasion two good friends of mine
> Did meete at meate, a Lawyer and Divine:
> Both having eaten well to helpe digestion,
> To this Divine, the lawyer put this question:
> When *Lazarus* in grave foure dayes did stay,
> Where was his soule? in heaven, or hell I pray?

> Was it in hell? Thence no redemption is.
> And if in heaven: would Christ abate his blisse?
> Sir, said the Preacher, for a short digression,
> First, answere me one point, in your profession:
> If so his heyres and he had falne to strife,
> Whose was the land, if he came backe to life?
> This latter question mov'd them all to lafter,
> And so they drunke one to another after.

Here the style is easy, full, comfortable: there is little attempt at elision or compression. The epigram does not turn on a final, witty couplet, but continues after the Preacher's answer to dwell on the hilarity that follows. The conclusion is inclusive and symmetrical, in contrast to the satirical epigrams, which deflate an opponent and reveal the superiority of the speaker. Essentially there are still two steps to the development—one conundrum capped by another— but some lines setting the scene introduce the conundrums and a couplet of narrative completion closes the epigram.

No. 184, "Against Lying *Lynus*," is an example of the satirical type:

> I wonder *Lynus*, what thy tongue doth ayle,
> That though I flatter thee, thou still doost raile?
> Thou think'st, I ly, perhaps thou think'st most true:
> Yet to so gentle lyes, pardon is due.
> A lie, wel told, to some tastes is restoritie;
> Besides, we Poets lie by good authoritie.
> But were all lying Poetry, I know it,
> *Lynus* would quickly prove a passing Poet.

A good deal of the interest and energy of the epigram comes from its double audience: the speaker has one eye on Lynus, and one on an appreciative public. The argument develops in brusque reflections, turning the idea of lying this way and that until the unexpected conclusion, which is nevertheless revealed as the implicit destination of all that has gone before. From flattery as lying, white ("gentle") lies, and lying as poetic fiction, a trap is constructed and then sprung on Lynus in the final couplet, where the notion that poets are liars is inverted to make all liars poets. The satisfying venom of this couplet, hurrying to its climax of alliterative "p"s, illustrates the saltiness Harington required for the epigram to make

it last. It is more literary than no. 65 ("Don Pedro")—it is too
long to be passed on as gossip—and more dramatic than no. 142
("Lazarus"), since it creates the characters of a caustic speaker and
his victim, and some suspense in the lithe turns of the argument.

A last example will serve to illustrate further the formal variety
of Harington's collection. No. 260 is called "Of the warres in
Ireland" ("Bonny Clabo" here is sour buttermilk; "sparvers" are
canopies):[19]

> I prays'd the speech, but cannot now abide it,
> That war is sweet, to those that have not try'd it:
> For I haue prov'd it now, and plainely see't,
> It is so sweet, it maketh all things sweet.
> At home Canarie wines and Greeke grow lothsome:
> Here milke is Nectar, water tasteth toothsome.
> There without bak't, rost, boyld, it is no cheere.
> Bisket we like, and Bonny Clabo heere.
> There we complaine of one reare rosted chicke:
> Heere viler meat, worse cookt, ne're makes me sicke.
> At home in silken sparvers, beds of Downe,
> We scant can rest, but still tosse up and downe:
> Here I can sleepe, a saddle to my pillow,
> A hedge the Curtaine, Canopy a Willow.
> There if a child but cry, oh what a spite!
> Heere we can brooke three larums in one night.
> There homely roomes must be perfum'd with Roses:
> Here match and powder ne're offends our noses.
> There from a storme of raine we run like Pullets:
> Heere we stand fast against a showre of bullets.
> Lo then how greatly their opinions erre,
> That thinke there is no great delight in warre:
> > But yet for this (sweet warre) Ile be thy debter,
> > I shall for ever love my home the better.

Erasmus had written an essay on the tag *Dulce bellum inexpertis* in
his *Adagia,* and it was a favorite of the Renaissance Humanists;[20]
Harington's epigram is built on a confrontation between this saying
and his own experience in the Irish wars. The theme is plainly stated
in the opening lines; for the rest, the reader follows an additive
series of illustrations, a succession of pairs of homely details. Indeed,
Harington's homemade quality, presenting his materials for what
they are, is obvious here, yet the commonplace subject matter

straightforwardly treated retains its interest, with variations on the basic contrast pointed by the rhymes (pillow/willow, pullets/bullets). Everyday materials are appropriate, after all, to the testing of a humanist tag about inexperience against experience.

Satiric Portraits

It was common practice among the English satirists of the 1590s to give their targets Latin names. Equally common was a denial like Martial's that the names referred to any particular person. Thomas Lodge and Thomas Bastard made the retort that anyone who claimed he was attacked in their satires was simply showing his own guilty conscience. Sir John Davies declared that anyone who thinks his epigrams are directed at any one individual "knowes not what an Epigramme doth meane: / Which Taxeth under a particular name, / A generall vice that merits publique blame."[21] Joseph Hall's editor, Arnold Davenport, who investigated Hall's attacks on the poet "Labeo" in his *Virgidemiarum* (1597–98), concluded that no one figure could be identified with the name. Hall seems to have had at least two contemporary poets in mind.[22]

Curiously, Harington does not claim that his Latin names are types or vices rather than individuals. In no. 423, "Of the objects of his satire," he responds to a lord who has pressed him "To know the secret drift of mine entent / In these my pleasent lynes, and who are meant / By *Cinna, Lynus, Lesbia,* and the rest." Harington replies with a genetic analogy: the wit that mothered them would rather not acknowledge their fathers' names now, though some of them "father themselves so shrewdly / That who gat some of them may soone be guest."

Humez's study of Harington's use of names from Martial shows that Harington took fifteen names from the Roman poet but built his own characters on them, using epigrams from different characters in Martial for his own creations and dividing the epigrams of a single Martial character among several of his own.[23] There are more than thirty characters in all with Latin names in Harington's collection, and twenty or so that appear more than once. Most give every appearance of representing a single, living person. As McClure says, Martial is often followed with only a name changed, apparently because that name had already been given "to a living person known to his readers."[24]

Harington has a name of his own, Lepidus (no. 219). Some progress has been made in identifying the others: Lynus, the character who appears most often, is the poet Barnabe Barnes. Peleus is Sir Matthew Arundell, as a reference to him in the *Metamorphosis* shows. Sir John Davies and Harington both attack Raleigh under the name of Paulus.[25] Two candidates have been suggested for Galla, who is reported to have married a "lofty prelate" in no. 366.[26]

The most vivid portrait in Harington's gallery is of Sir Walter Raleigh or Paulus. In one epigram he is "my friend *Paulus*" (no. 15); in another he expects Harington to be his follower now that he is "a great man," but he is too much in awe of Harington's enemies to offer any protection (no. 22). In a third he attacks Harington's life of private recreation and contemplation as a "Paradice of fooles," while he himself (in Harington's retort) finds only hell in his journeys to far-off places (no. 61). Another tells of a shared ride to Rochester, bantering about worn-out horses and bald heads (no. 79). Paulus robs the Spanish of gold, while Harington steals poetic conceits from the Romans (no. 126). One version of no. 257 quotes Paulus as a "table friend," someone attracted by lavish hospitality rather than a true friend to the provider of it.[27]

Raleigh was not the first to bring tobacco to England, but he was its most notorious user and promoter and traded in it up to his death in 1618.[28] There are glimpses in the epigrams of Raleigh swaggering through London, crying up tobacco while he has some to sell, buying it "At Tippling-houses, where he eates and drinks, / That every roome straight of Tobacco stinks." When he has sold all his he will cry it down again (no. 134). In no. 315 he is abasing himself before the queen, so that "While he dawbes his speech with flatteries plaster, / And calls himselfe her slave, he growes our Master." His private life is a matter of open scandal: he has a wife, though he has never been married, just as Caius is a father though he has not begotten any children (no. 410). With unconsciously accurate wording Paulus advertises open house at Christmas "for all of both the sexes," i.e., for homosexuals ("Hermaphrodites": no. 386). Worst of all is his atheism. He declares that the heavens are empty and gods do not exist; for proof he points to the fact that while he blasphemes like this he lives in luxury, in "earthly blisse" (no. 110). He derides the idea of saints or angels ever appearing on earth, and Harington drily accepts his proof that wherever he goes Paulus "A Fiend worse then himselfe, shall never see" (no. 122).

Among the characters in the epigrams who have not been identified is "Leda." She is often in the writer's company. Harington
seems fascinated by her extravagant posturings. She is certain she
is of the Elect, and therefore pampers her body, which she calls
"the Temple of the Holy Ghost," with food and clothes (Harington
is sure that all she is doing is feeding and clothing "a Synagogue
of Sathan" [no. 90]). In another epigram, he says he has been asked
what sect she inclines to; she is no recusant, since she makes light
of Lent and fast-days; she is no Protestant, since her faith is so
suspect she cannot hope to be saved by it. Harington concludes,
punning on the names of contemporary religious sects, that she is
a Brownist for the color of her face and breast, and Family of Love
for the rest of her body (no. 102).[29]

Leda has some criticisms of her own to make: she complains that
Harington's epigrams have made people suspicious he is a Puritan
(no. 157); his mentioning Moses in an epigram is sacrilege, "byble
stories joynd with bables" (no. 362); she does not approve of the
"Ryding-rhymes" or rhyming couplets in his epigrams (no. 245).
No. 332 reflects on the rivalry between Leda and Mall. Leda, come
to take the waters in Bath in hopes of becoming fertile, wears the
kind of flamboyant finery Mall eschews, though she is better entitled
to wear it than Leda. The epigram is titled "The Author to his
Wife":

> Your maid *Brunetta* you with newes acquaints,
> How *Leda,* (whom, her husband wanting issue,
> Brought erst to Bath, our pilgrimage of Saints)
> Weares her gowne velvet, kirtle, cloth of tissue,
> A figur'd Sattin petticote Carnation,
> With six gold parchment laces all in fashion.
> Yet neither was Dame *Leda* nobler borne,
> Nor dranke in Gossips cup by Sov'raigne sent,
> Nor ever was her Highnes woman sworne,
> Nor doth her husband much exceed in rent.
>   Then *Mall,* be proud, that thou maist better weare them.
>   And I more proud, thou better dost forbeare them.

Characters emerge from the scattered epigrams about them vigorously individualized by their hypocrisy: "pure" Cinna boasts that
he belongs to the Elect, scorns the superstitions of the Church of
England, lives "lewdly," duels self-righteously; he married a maid-

servant straight after burying his wife.[30] Cosmus takes bribes from all sides and attacks churchmen with multiple offices while he piles up civil offices himself; he is a miser for all his wealth and promises to live like a lord, finish his building, and keep proper house "after awhile."[31] Marcus feasts extravagantly and wants to borrow money and plate to keep up his state; when his carousing in "March Beere and Sacke" makes him dizzy, he blames it on the pipe of tobacco he smoked.[32]

Not surprisingly, the characters who appear under their own names are generally honored rather than satirized, friends like Sir Hugh Portman, noble connections like Essex, and fellow-poets like Heywood, Davies, Daniel, and Bastard. Thomas Nashe and Robert Joyner are attacked by name, however, and some figures from the past like Bishop Bonner and Sir John Raynsford are mentioned in uncomplimentary fashion. The figures who appear most often as themselves are of course Mall, Harington's wife, and Lady Rogers, his mother-in-law.

Conclusion

When Thomas Park came to edit the *Nugae Antiquae* selection from the Harington papers in 1804, he found the epigrams had little to recommend them, "unless for the purpose of contemporary illustration."[33] T. S. Eliot's comment, in a review of 1927, was that the epigrams "illustrate well the mentality of a cultivated and wholly uninspired country gentleman of the time."[34] Published criticism since Eliot has confined itself to distinctly qualified commendations of Harington's efforts.[35] Part of the problem in doing justice to the epigrams is that they belong to a backwater of literary history: not obviously a part of the urban, intellectual satire of the 1590s like Sir John Davies's, not representing a robust classicism like Ben Jonson's, they are a heterogeneous blend of idiosyncratic imitations of Martial, traditional jests and wordplays, and ready-made materials coming directly from Harington's own experience. Moreover, the very fact that Jonson, second only to Shakespeare among the commanding figures of the English literary Renaissance, took up the form, doomed Harington to an inevitable and invidious comparison. Jonson himself told Drummond that Harington's epigrams were no epigrams at all, but "Narrations"—too prosaic, and too explicit, to merit the title.[36] To judge Harington's work by the standard of Jonson's tensely shaped utterances, his ruthless armored assault on the gull and the knave, and his measured praise of the virtuous is to miss the attractive qualities of inclusiveness and informality, the balance of tolerance and perspicaciousness, that Harington achieves in his easy, confidential manner.

The epigrammatic form as Martial developed it belonged to a self-consciously low style: casual and colloquial rather than merely plain, it defined itself by ironic contrast with the grander modes of epic and tragedy. Its special territory was the failings and foibles of mankind, or, better, that gap between a corrupt human nature and the pretensions and aspirations of the individual, which has always invited satire. This combination of the low style and a characteristically sardonic attitude served Harington well. His homely materials, the reported reactions of his real-world audience, and his "flat" style declare the allegiance of the epigrams to the world of experience rather than to the world of art. In the medium of the epigram, experience crystallizes into an attitude, precipitated by borrowings from Martial, from the store of classical adages, from folk sayings, and from a repertoire of wordplays and conceits from miscellaneous sources. The characters of his epigrams are translated from the domain of immediate, formless experience into a parallel region where they have recognizable roles and permit clear-cut reactions. The Latin names of his satiric portraits are the best index of this translation from gossip to the threshold of fiction, but something like the same process occurs even when individuals keep their English proper names.

Although the epigrammatic mode typically suspects moralizing, and Harington's favorite targets are the self-righteously "pure" Puritans, certain values are implicit. This is perhaps Harington's special contribution to the form: his genial satire defends a conservative, Christian civilization, acknowledging man's sinfulness while attacking hypocrisy in general and abuses like corruption in the Church in particular. The stout final couplets of the epigrams measure a distance in values as well as in genius from the cynical elegance of Martial's deft closures.

Chapter Five

Translations, Paraphrases, and Prose Tracts

The Englishman's Doctor

At the end of the second section of *The Metamorphosis of Ajax,* Harington introduces "certaine autenticall rules, out of a provinciall Councell of Physitions" (156). The rules are from a medieval poem, *Regimen Sanitatis Salernitanum,* "a series of wise maxims written in plain language on the care of the health" deriving from the school of medicine at Salernum, near Naples. It survived into the Renaissance in hundreds of editions and manuscript copies, and seems to have attained the status of a standard textbook on health.[1]

In the *Metamorphosis* Harington quotes it on his favorite topics of flatulence and the ventilation of privies, and uses the opening lines of the poem and its advice on pears and apples (157–59). In 1607 his verse translation of the whole poem appeared, anonymously, as *The Englishmans docter. Or, the Schoole of Salerne.* This was the first translation of the poem into English; further editions appeared up to 1624.[2]

Harington's translation seems to be based on a version related to a text of the *Regimen* commented on by Arnold of Villa Nova, which is about 360 lines long (some versions were more than a thousand lines long).[3] It is divided into ten-line stanzas, seventy in all. Harington's practice was to add two, three, or four lines to most of the stanzas to fill out a translation of the original by way of commentary. To the warning against keeping in wind, for example, he adds four lines on the Emperor Claudius's edict making it lawful to break wind in company (79). The edict had already been mentioned in the *Metamorphosis* (122), and there are many things in *The Englishman's Doctor* familiar from this work, and from others—a joke on leanness and leaning caused by drink, for instance, recalls one of the epigrams (84; no. 175). References to Martial and Horace are interpolated occasionally as urbane asides, like this one on the virtues of drinking wine at dinner:

> For water and small beere we make no question,
> Are enemies to health and good digestion:
> And *Horace* in a verse of his rehearses,
> That *Water-drinkers* never make good verses.
>
> (93)

Two added lines on temperance modify the strictly practical approach of the original: "But gainst all surfets, vertues school hath taught / To make the gift of temperance a shield" (88).

There are also interpolated comments reflecting on natural philosophy, like this comment on the link between humours and behavior: "Complexions cannot vertue breed or vice, / Yet may they unto both give inclination" (134). Other additions belong in a category of miscellaneous country lore, pithy sayings, and worldly wisdom: a note that the mallard provides good sport but bad eating (94); brief explorations of the punning possibilities of the names of the herbs sage and rue (112, 114); and a comment that the translator is readier to wear a leek on St. David's Day than eat one on St. David's Eve (122).

Harington's *Englishman's Doctor* is thus a characteristic blend of workmanlike verse, pithily proverbial expression, and scattered allusions to his favorite classical authors. To these are added anecdotes and asides generally arising from plays on words and relying on an earthy understanding of human nature. In a later edition of the *Regimen,* Philemon Holland translates the lines "Si tibi deficiunt medici, medici tibi fiant / Haec tria, mens laeta, requies, moderata diaeta" thus: "When Phisicke needes, let these thy Doctors be, / Good diet, quiet thoughts, heart mirthfull, free."[4] Harington's version is: "Use three Physicions still; first Doctor *Quiet,* / Next Doctor *Merry-man,* and Doctor *Dyet*" (75). He has made use of a personifying proverb to make the instruction direct and memorable;[5] his lines have a certain rustic heartiness, where Holland's more polished lines suggest a gentleman's ease. Harington's couplet caught the eye of Robert Burton, who reminded the reader that mirth "is one of the three Salernitan doctors, Dr. Merryman, Dr. Diet, Dr. Quiet, which cures all diseases."[6]

The Psalms

Harington's last venture in verse was his metrical paraphrase of the Book of Psalms. Putting the psalms into verse was a commonplace literary exercise for Englishmen after the Reformation; hundreds of poets, good and bad, tried their hands at complete or partial metrical psalters in the period.[7] Harington's particular model was the psalter begun by Sir Philip Sidney and completed by his sister Mary. He owned manuscript copies of the Sidneys' psalter and commended it more than once; in his own paraphrase, he imitated their extravagant display of metrical virtuosity and borrowed words and phrases from their version.[8] The Sidneys' model, in turn, was the French translation by Marot and Beza, which was inspired by Calvin's belief in congregational singing. It used a wide variety of stanzas and meters and set the psalms to a range of different tunes.[9] In versifying the psalms in conspicuously varied verse forms the Sidneys departed from the standard English verse psalter of the time, the Sternhold and Hopkins "Old Version." This put the entire psalter into couplets of four and three iambic feet, "fourteeners," which became known as the "Old Meter."[10]

Like the Sidneys, Harington used the Prayer Book psalter for the basis of his paraphrase, supplemented by the Geneva translation, which he had elsewhere called "the best translacion read in owr Churche."[11] In the Bodleian manuscript of his complete psalter, each psalm is designated for use in morning or evening prayer on a given day in a thirty-day cycle, as prescribed in the Book of Common Prayer.

The most striking aspect of Harington's psalter is its metrical variation. At various times, he uses stanzas of anywhere between three and fourteen lines, and lines of three, four, and five (mostly iambic) feet. His rhyme schemes are predominantly based on alternate rhyme *(a b a b)*, but so interspersed with pair-rhymes *(a a)*, inset-rhymes *(a b b a)* and irregular forms that very few are repeated. Twenty-one of the twenty-two parts of Psalm 119, for example, are cast into sonnet form (the odd one has only thirteen lines); there are seventeen different rhyme-schemes among them.

At their worst, Harington's psalms are mere hack-work, the words of the original obviously filled out and rearranged to fit the verse forms. At their best, in jaunty or muted celebration, in railing or heartsick lament, they create a distinctive and energetic voice. Psalm

23 lies somewhere between the two extremes, with occasional infelic-
ities but also sustaining a certain dignity (these are stanzas 1, 2,
and 5):

> The Lord is sheppard I his sheepe
>   himselfe both rulde and fedd me
> In pastures greene hee did me keepe
>   to Christall springs he led me
>
> His name releiv'd me wanting breath
>   and plast in path of comfort
> that though I walke in waies of death
>   my soule hath noe discomfort
>
> Thie mercie makes me thus to spend
>   my daies in sweete simplicity
> And manie more thou maist me lend
>   to live in like felicity
>
> (fol. 13v)

This muted, resigned note recalls the devotional stanzas Harington added to his *Orlando Furioso*. The beginning of Psalm 33 is a
fine example of the more joyful voice of Harington's version:

> Bee thanckfull and reioyce
>   to Iust men ioy belongs
> Praise god with harpe & voyce
>   and tune your strings to songs
> with courage strayne your cheerefull throats
>   to chaunt aloud well tuned notes.
>
> His words most trew doe prove
>   his works are faithful still
> He iudgements iust doth love
>   his favors earth doth fill
> His word did make ye heav'ns soe hie
>   and all the hoasts of starry skie
>
> (fol. 18v)

Harington seems equally at home when the Psalmist heaps im-
precations on his enemies. The self-pity of one who feels he has had
evil returned for good, and the uninhibited cursing that follows, is
vigorously expressed in this pair of stanzas from Psalm 109:

> Their lipps doe fayne and glose
>   still thwarting all I say
> I looke for love they hate as foes
>   yet I for them doe pray
>
> Sith for good turnes and love
>   hee renders hate and evill
> set thou some Tyrant him above
>   and some malitious devill
>   (fol. 68)

In the Penitential Psalms, the venom is turned inward, to the Psalmist's own sinfulness. Psalm 51 illustrates this aspect of Harington's psalter, as well as his handling of the longer line:

> Have mercie Lord of thine aboundant grace
> forgive my guilt that greiveth all my sences
>   blott out my blame my faults record deface
> with mercies mayne remitt my mayne offences
> O wash o rence my soule without within
> to make me cleane from this my filthie synne
>   (fols. 30v–31)

Looking through Harington's psalter as a whole, it is clear that rhyme is his main formal means. It makes for an elaborateness which is occasionally distracting; double rhymes, for instance, risk a bathetic effect, as in this final couplet from Psalm 66: "Hee rules the world his eye is each where serching / & pulls the prowd unfaithfull from his perching" (fol. 38v). Triple rhymes often come too close to being identical, as in the "simplicity/felicity" rhyme in Psalm 23. On the other hand, conspicuous rhymes are skillfully used in Psalm 33, quoted above, where their chiming is part of the celebratory music of the psalm. Rhyming triolets also put conspicuous rhyming to good use, producing the breathless suspense of an ingenious juggling feat. Psalm 133 is a good example:

> Behould a Ioy that doth excell
>   when brothers love their brothers well
>   and doe in peace togeather dwell

Tis like that ioyce of fragrant fume
with which the Preists alone presume
their hallowed garments to perfume
(fols. 83–83v)

Harington's psalms also depend heavily on alliteration. The effect can be slightly comic, as when the just man "pincheth not the pupills portion" (fol. 8; Psalm 15), or can rise to a pointed conclusion, as in Psalm 16's description of the bliss hereafter, "where thie right hand shall hould me in thy presence / the princely place of our perpetuall pleasance" (fol. 8v). A sweetly balanced group of alliterations forms the close of Psalm 107: "the wise will way these works, & thereby measure / the graces great of our most loving Lord" (fol. 67v). The technique can intensify a mood to the point of melodrama:

From horror huge of darke dispaire and deepe
my soule hath cryde with seas of synne surrownded
oh heare the voyce that in thine eare hath sownded
both heare and heed and seeme not Lord asleepe
(fol. 82; Psalm 130)

It can also introduce a certain quaintness, as when "In rifts of rocks the runing Rabetts rest" (fol. 63; Psalm 104).

Patterning by parallelisms and refrains is common in the psalms,[12] and Harington incorporates this into his version. The thirteen quatrains of Psalm 136 each contain two lines of refrain. These are the first two:

O praise our God that us doth love
because his mercie ever lasteth
Praise God of gods all Gods above
because his bownty neaver wasteth
O praise this Lord of other Lords
because his love for ever lasteth
whose only works deserve records
because his bownty never wasteth
(fol. 84v)

The last verses of Psalms 42 and 43 are almost identical in the Prayer Book psalter, and Harington copies this feature in his version.

Enjambments are rare and generally awkward in Harington's verse; his iambic, end-stopped lines always run the risk of seeming merely piled one on top of the other, making wearyingly jerky progress. A stanza from Psalm 39 will illustrate:

> I did a while my speach refraine
>   as well fro good as ill
> Yea though to me it were a paine
>   I silent stood and still
>   (fol. 23v)

On the other hand, the same pattern of a four-stressed line alternating with a three-stressed one can produce a pleasant dying fall, as in Psalm 141:

> I crye and lift my voyce to thee
>   to thine all seeing eyes
> As Incence my devotion bee
>   or evening sacrifice
>
> Set watch and ward at either lipp
>   least there the tempter lurking
> my hart to evill thoughts may slipp
>   my hands to wicked working
>   (fols. 87–87v)

The difference is in the rhymes—less awkward throughout in the second example, and alternating masculine with feminine; and in the more restrained use of the first-person pronoun. Psalm 141 uses the shorter lines for sense-units in apposition rather than for material carrying forward the sentence. In this way the jog-trot, sing-song rhythm is turned to good use in plaintive repetition.

Harington often brings a contemporary range of reference to the psalms by his vocabulary. In Psalm 50 there is a flurry of legal terminology, "evidence," "tryall," "Iudgement," "verdict," "plaintiffe Iudge," and "Arrerages" on a debt (fols. 30–30v). In Psalm 55 the Prayer Book psalter's ". . . my companion: my guide, and mine owne familiar friend. / Wee tooke sweete counsell together: and walked in the house of God as friends" (verses 14 and 15) has become

>   . . . my frend esteemed best of all
>   my pewfellow companion & my guyde
>   with whome to Church I often did repair
>   with whome I ioynd in conferrence & prai'r
>   (fol. 33)

In Psalm 69 "the dronkards make songs upon me" (verse 12) is paraphrased as "to my reproch the drunkards publish rymes / in tavernes bace and ordinary Tables" (fol. 41). Harington's own preoccupations are echoed in the lexicon of his paraphrases: the metaphor of the "baited hook," familiar from *Orlando Furioso,* in Psalms 69 and 141 (fols. 41, 87v); the sin of "partial passion" in the king (fol. 42v; Psalm 72); and the "pleasant fountains" of Psalm 98 (fol. 59v). This is a Jacobean, even a colloquial David, whose song is a "Ditty" (fol. 28; Psalm 46). His God has foiled those whose "Engins crafty" seek to trap the just man's soul, so that "the birder mist his pray" (fol. 80v; Psalm 124).[13]

Harington also tends to elaborate the metaphors in his original. In this he is following the Sidneys' psalter. In Psalm 139, as J. C. A. Rathmell explains, the Countess of Pembroke drew on Calvin's commentary to elaborate the metaphors of embroidery and craftsman's shop for God's part in the creation of the unborn baby.[14] Here Harington follows closely, using the phrases "th'mbrodered works" and "in darkest shopp" (fol. 86v; Psalm 139). Elsewhere he is more independent. A sample from Psalm 107 will illustrate further the relationship among the three versions. The Prayer Book psalter has: "They that go downe to the sea in ships: and occupie their business in great waters. / These men see the works of the Lord: and his wonders in the deepe" (verses 23 and 24). The Countess of Pembroke refashions this into a fuller, more explicit meditation on the works of the Lord:

>   How many mounting winged tree
>   For traffique, leave retiring land,
>   And on huge waters busied be,
>   Which bancklesse flow on endlesse sand!
>   These, these indeed, well understand,
>   Enform'd by their feare-open ey,
>   The wonders of Jehovas hand
>   While on the waves they rocking ly.
>   (ll. 57–64)

Harington borrows the metaphor of the "winged tree," but otherwise stays closer to the Prayer Book psalter; he relies on alliteration and emphatic adjectives, where the countess depends on a controlled meditative rhythm:

> Whoe post to seas on horse of winged tree
>   and trudge for trade beyond ye saltish wave
> In clowdy deepe his wonders cleerely see
>   Where blustring storm & raging tempests rave
>   (fol. 66v)

There are many examples of what Schmutzler calls "Harington at his poetic worst" in the psalms. There are times when the material is obviously twisted and padded merely to fill out a meter and rhyme scheme, where stanzas and psalms simply end, as though suspended, or halt with a bathetic abruptness. At times Harington's plainness is no better than lifelessness, and occasionally a dreary literariness muffles the impact. Yet his psalter does have its successes, as we have seen. At times his modest strengths as a poet, familiar from his *Orlando Furioso,* come together to make an appealing harmony, in which a jauntiness, and a homemade quality bordering on naiveté, as well as a grasp of stout poetic tools like alliteration and conspicuous rhymes, play their part.

The achievement of the psalter is a respectable one, even if Harington's own boast that few divines could have written such poetry, and few poets such pure divinity, seems a doubtful one today.[15] He may justifiably be allotted at least a portion of the commendation the Psalmist gave himself in Psalm 45 (this is Harington's version):

> Myne hart indights noe slight or vulgar song
>   my ditties frame is of and for a king
> like pen of scribe most prompt my flowing tongue
>   Yeilds streames of praise, as from a plenteous spring
>   (fol. 27)

Early Prose Tracts

The earliest among Harington's surviving tracts and discourses is probably *A Discourse shewing that Elyas must personally come before the Day of Judgement.* The tract is a contribution to the controversy over the return of Elias (Elijah) to prepare for the Second Coming prophesied in Malachi 4:5–6. Difficulty was caused by the fact that in the New Testament Jesus says that Elijah has already come, apparently in reference to John the Baptist's ministry (Matthew 17:10–13). The Patristic view was that John the Baptist was not literally Elijah returned but that he came in the spirit of Elijah.[16] This is the belief that Harington is defending in the *Discourse*. He quotes St. Augustine and other Church Fathers to support it and discusses two further scriptural passages.

According to Aharon Wiener, the belief that Elijah would return to herald the Second Coming (a belief known as "parousia") "disappeared almost completely after about the beginning of the middle ages." Harington seems therefore to be defending an old-fashioned doctrine.[17] In the *Metamorphosis* he denies that the doctrine is a "Popish" opinion (262); however, his adverse comments in the *Discourse* are directed mainly at the opposite persuasion, the Puritans. He takes issue on the interpretation of Malachi 4 with Peter Martyr, generally a guide to Protestant orthodoxy (285–86),[18] derides one of "pure stamp," i.e., of the Puritan faction, for interpreting the two witnesses of Revelation 11 as the Old and New Testaments (297–98), and disputes the opinion of "Owr honest and not suttle, but simple" John Foxe that the two witnesses are John Hus and Jerome of Prague (296–97).

Harington is conservative, too, in giving credence to traditions of belief that do not have the authority of the Scriptures; he admits that they do not "bynd owr beleefe as infallible treweths, yet they lead it as strong prejudyces, and, as it is fondness to affyrm them to ernestly, so it is rashness to reject them to contemtuouwsly." The assumption of our Lady is one of these (299–300). Here there is a careful distinction between those things that a Christian is bound to believe and those where some dispute is possible; he puts the subject of his discourse firmly in the second category right from the start (282).

Harington argues for an interpretation of the Scriptures restricted to "the playn and naturall sence" (283). The surest guides to this are the earliest commentators, who are "furthest of[f] from the wofull schismes of this tyme, and freest from all partiallityes": that is, the commentaries of the Church Fathers (293). He is impatient with interpretations that read figures, tropes, and allegories into the literal sense of the text, though in one instance he has to argue that "it is usuall in the holye skripture not only for one place to have more meanings then one, but allso for one prophecye to signifye more tymes than one" (288).[19]

Harington's *A Treatise on Playe* (ca. 1597) is intended "to establish an honor and order" in gambling, "which in wise mens opinions is now both dishonorably and disorderly abused," especially at court (187).[20] The treatise goes on to distinguish the various forms of "playe": devotional (like singing psalms), wanton ("enterludes, tumblers, jesting fooles, and scoffers, masking and dawncing"), and games involving betting (either purely games of chance, or those requiring mental and bodily skill: 188–95).

It is this third kind of play that Harington is concerned with in his tract. He approaches it as a physician might approach a disease, locating its causes in three "evill affections of the mynde," sloth, pride, and greed, and proposing a cure that will moderate rather than eradicate these factors. This cure, which he develops as he analyzes the three causes, is to play for modest stakes using money in high denominations as chips (195–220). He would have the great of the kingdom keep up an "honorable shew,"

play on a velvet carpet, handle nothing but golde, talke of nothing but pownds, and yet to venter no more than they may with their honors trewly pay, and with theyr ease willingly spare. (206–7)

Harington then shows that gambling does not provide prosperity; the professional "gamster" who gets a good living in the dicing-house and keeps it is as rare as a black swan; the dicing-box is the ruin of "infinit young gentlemen" (244–27). The last part of the discourse dilates on three particular aspects of the usefulness of Harington's invention of "counterfayt play." Those addicted to playing for large sums will be weaned off it in gradual fashion; the widespread use of the system would reduce heavy gambling by a kind of debasement of the currency; and it would mean less bad temper at the gambling table (227–32).

Harington addresses himself particularly in all this to the court. Individuals from the court circle serve as examples, like Hatton (210) and Pembroke (220), or as targets, like the patron of play labeled "the irreverent doctor Fawstus," who also appears in many epigrams (208). At times, indeed, Harington's tract sounds much like a courtesy book. Play is useful because the presence-chamber should not be left empty half the day, and it will keep the players and spectators occupied. Harington is not one of those who would banish all comfort and recreation from the court, as some of the older servants would (200). After all, "the stately pallaces, goodly and many chambers, fayr gallerys, large gardens, sweet walkes, that princes with magnificent cost do make" show that they desire their followers' "ease, content and pleasure," as well as their own (201–2).

Further comment reminiscent of the distinctions and discriminations of the courtesy book defines the recreations proper to the gentleman: "to be plesawnt conseyted, to be actyve and musicall, are cowrtly and liberall quallyties," but "for noble personages to become jesters, tumblers, and pypers, is hateful, fond, and dishonourable" (194). All cheating, all "base-mynded shifts and cosenages" should be scorned by the gentleman, and his play should never provoke "unseemly or untemperat passions" (212). A gentleman should never "chafe at his ill luck," nor should gentlemen "beate theyr fystes on the boord, flinge the cardes under table," as some of them do even in the presence-chamber (231).

In his treatise Harington defines his own attitude to gambling by contrast with those "severe and stoycall" reformers who would banish it altogether. His own opinion is that it is "at the worst, tollerable; for the most part, indifferent; and in some sort, commendable" (186–87). This tolerant, sympathetic attitude informs Harington's guiding metaphor of humours and disease. Gambling is a kind of infection, and one Harington himself has only barely escaped (195). Its causes he has found by examining his own imperfections, as well as those of other men; the cure must be like a good doctor's medicine, "not quite to take away the humors, but only to restrayne the dangerows overflowing thearof" (196). After all, play has its uses: "recreation after study, ease after payne, rest after labour, is very necessary" (186).

Harington's diagnosis and proposed cure are based on a shrewd analysis of human nature. His is not a tract railing at other men's sins, but an understanding insider's attempt to regulate abuses of an activity he admits is in itself neither good nor bad, abuses rooted in human failings he knows he shares himself. His powers of observations are evident in his picture of the aristocratic gamblers who play with a magnificent carelessness for thousands of pounds before an admiring audience, but who then (once out of the public eye) will cry poor to a mercer over a debt of ten pounds and take an agent to task for engaging laborers at eightpence a day instead of sevenpence (204–5). It is pride that leads to these ridiculous inconsistencies; men always want to be taken for better than they are:

> wee use much bumbastings and quiltings to seeme better formed, better showldered, smaller wasted, and fuller thyght, then wee are; wee barbe and shave ofte, to seeme yownger than wee are; we use perfumes both inward and outward, to seeme sweeter then wee be; corkt shoes to seeme taller then wee be; wee use cowrtuows salutations to seem kinder then wee bee. . . . (209)

Tract on the Succession to the Crown (1602)

Harington's discourse on the succession is dated 1602, the year before Elizabeth's death. Public discussion of the question of who was to succeed the queen was dangerous; an act of 1571 forbade the publication of any claims to the succession other than those approved by Parliament, and Peter Wentworth, whom Harington quotes, was imprisoned twice in the 1590s for his *Pithie Exhortation* on the topic, and for involving himself in discussions about it.[21] Harington says the queen will hear no talk about the succession because she fears that if there is free discussion and publication on the question of "whose was the best title after hirs, some would be ready to affirme that title to be good afore hers." Moreover, such talk was a reminder of mortality: "she would not have hir wynding sheet sett up afore hir face." Harington himself is in some trepidation about writing his tract but reassures himself he is not breaking any law if he does not publish it, as he never did (39–40).[22]

As he notes in the *Tract,* he had been involved in the question at the time of the Bond of Association, much earlier in his career. In 1602, with Queen Elizabeth's reign clearly drawing to a close, he was making his support for James as her successor very plain. When he sent the Scottish king an emblematic lantern in 1602, he cast himself as the Good Thief, asking to be remembered when his Lord came into his Kingdom; in the *Tract on the Succession,* he offers himself as John the Baptist, "a well-willer and forerunner *to him whose shoe latchet I am not worthie to unloose*" (95).

The main objections to James were the facts that he was a foreigner and (for Catholics) that he was a Protestant. Harington's *Tract* sets out to refute them. It treats the religious dimension of the succession question as the most important; Harington's strategy is to address the three main religious groups (Protestant, Puritan, Catholic) in turn to overcome their objections to James as the next King of England. His aim is a consensus founded on the separation of religion and politics in which all sides will accept James as Elizabeth's successor. A policy of religious toleration is also put forward on the basis of this principle.

The *Tract* starts with a rhetorical problem: it is Harington's observation that very few speakers in his day, however gifted and well-instructed they may be, actually succeed in persuading their audience to believe them. The reason seems to be that the age is particularly prone to suspicions of partiality. To overcome this obstacle he has chosen to quote from writers from each of the three religious factions on the question of the succession, writers writing in other languages and to other nations, and very different in their views, "yet all in this one poynt admirably concurring" (3).

The Duke of Somerset's address "To the Nobles and Counsellors, People and Comonalitie of Scotland" (1548)[23] is quoted first, as an authoritative Protestant view. Somerset hoped to allay the fears of the Scots about the marriage, then projected, between Edward VI and Mary Queen of Scots. He reminded his audience that the marriage would mean an end to wars between the two countries, a new and invulnerable kingdom, and that England was offering a union rather than aiming at conquest; as token of this, he offered to change the name of the united kingdoms to Britain. All this Harington finds remarkably apt to the present situation, so apt that it might almost be a prophecy. He confesses how much he was moved by reading these prophetic passages; for all the skeptics' objections to prophecies, he finds almost everyone to be impressed by them. They are a reflection of the hand of Providence in human history, like the remarkable way the present situation has come about, in which the most direct living descendant of the English Henry VIII (besides Elizabeth) is the King of Scotland. It is "a work of the finger of God . . . in which the inscrutable judgementes of the most highest do . . . plainly appear" (16–19).

Harington next quotes the Puritan Peter Wentworth's discourse on the succession.[24] It urges that James is the natural heir to the crown, dismisses the impediment of his foreign birth, and shows that the act that followed the Bond of Association cleared James from complicity in his mother's attempts on the crown. He also has more

positive arguments for James's succession in the security and prosperity of the united kingdom that would result.

Harington then adds a chapter of his own in support of Wentworth's views. He dismisses the multiplicity of other candidates:
some he says were put forward by the Privy Council to counter-
balance the claims of Mary Queen of Scots in the days when she
was alive; others like Lady Arabella Stuart and a French claimant
have emerged more recently. He has reasons for distrusting all of
them, the more so because he is familiar with all the great figures
involved in the succession question. He has even discussed an episode
in the *Orlando* with Lady Arabella (44–45).

Harington then turns to the Papists, the most dangerous of the
three groups, as an embattled minority: they "are feared most,
because they feare most" (7). He quotes at length from the *Conference
about the Next Succession to the Crown of England* (1594), thought to
be by the Jesuit Robert Parsons, on aspects of Mary's claims that
(according to Harington) bear equally on her son's. These are legal
answers to the objection of Mary's foreign birth, and to her variance
from the Established Church in England. He also quotes his friend
Henry Constable (though not by name).[25] Constable had written as
a Catholic in support of the Huguenot Henry IV, arguing that his
accession to the French throne was the work of Providence, and that
toleration and compromise are possible in France in his reign. Harington eagerly takes up the argument that subjects must accept a
king different in religion from their own and applies it to the English
Catholics and to James as a future king of England. He shows, too,
that Constable's praise of Henry can be equally applied to James,
in the providential circumstances of his succession, in James's prow-
ess in letters matching Henry's in arms, in James's legitimate off-
spring matching Henry's illegitimate, and so on (71–72).

Harington next takes the opportunity to refute the general se-
ditiousness of Parsons's *Conference,* and its partiality toward the House
of York, on the basis (he admits) of notes made in Ireland from a
copy borrowed there (he says it is dangerous to ask for copies in
England). The peroration to this section is a prayer that James may
inherit all the good qualities of the united houses of York and
Lancaster, "the person and amiableness of Edward the Fourth, the
wisdome and providence of Henrie the Seaventh, the bounty and
royaltie of K. Henrie the Eight and his daughter Marié, the felicitie
and quiet daies and long life of Queen Elizabeth . . ." (81).

The eulogy of James that follows suggests that the Scottish king
is indeed fortunate. Having praised James under each of ten heads
in turn—with some general discussion of the virtues in question,
apparently particularly heartfelt in the case of the prince's liberality
to deserving subjects (85)—he adds remarks on James's happy al-
liance with Denmark through his wife, the Danish king's sister,
and on his two sons and daughter, who promise a secure succession.
As a final argument to convince his readers, he returns to the security
James would bring England as king by the union of the two kingdoms. He points out that this is especially necessary in the present
state of the nation, with costly wars in the Low Countries and a
dangerous rebellion in Ireland—moreover, an invasion from Scotland or Denmark, if any rival to James were to succeed Elizabeth,
would be difficult to repel. This note had been struck earlier in the
Tract: instability of any kind is to be feared in such a time as the
present,

> when malecontentes so abound in citie and countrye, when in the Court
> the comon phrase of old servantes is that their is no commiseracion of any
> man's distressed estate, that a few favourites gett all, that the nobilitie is
> depressed, the Clergy pilled [plundered] and contemned, forraine invasions
> expected, the treasure at home exhausted, the coyne in Ireland imbased,
> the gold of England transported, exactions doubled and trebled, and all
> honest heartes so troubled. . . . (76)

The last chapter of the *Tract* treats the religious position of contemporary England: how it has come about and how to deal with
its main problem, the Catholic minority (the Puritans, Harington
says, are thought to be decreasing in number and losing their friends
[6]). Harington's view of the religious question is based on the belief
that religious matters are a question for God and a man's conscience
(74). What the history of the English Reformation shows is that
doctrine was always mixed with politics, with self-interest; so it
was with Henry VIII's reformation, with the image-breakers in
Edward VI's time, and with the restoration of Catholicism under
Mary (98–100).

Only when "politique faction be devided frome Religion" will
reconciliation be possible (96). It is the Papists' practices against
the State that makes toleration impossible (7–8); before intrigues
involving Mary Queen of Scots began to threaten the nation's safety,

patriotism was not necessarily inseparable from Protestantism, and "religion brake not freindshipp, brake no allegeance, bard no good opinion" (103). What must be done is to stop punishing Catholics by law, and to divide matters of religion from matters of state (114); strict laws, making acts of religion treasons, only intensify the "sinister practises" of the persecuted group (104). Neither the burning in Queen Mary's time, nor the hanging in the present time, nor the use of both in Henry's time, has done any good at all (109).

Harington's own attempt at pacification is to give credit to all sides for their sincerity, since there are good men in all three camps (92). He urges that men cease to be so busy about each other's reformation, but concentrate on their own. As he had already said in the *Metamorphosis,* he is himself a "protesting Catholique Puritan":

. . . for the name Papist, Protestant, or Puritan, I finde them not in the Scripture, nor in any writer 1500 years after, and therefore I aunswer with a Father, *Christian* is my name, *Catholique* my surname, and this I hope is a sound aunswer, and will not be found fault with, as long as the preachers call the Queen defendresse of the true, auncient, catholique and Apostolique faith. (108)

Since it was not printed, and the activities of men like Robert Cecil brought about a peaceful transition of power to James when Elizabeth died in 1603,[26] Harington's eloquence on the question of the succession was never widely tested; it is interesting, however, that Robert Cecil himself had an epitome of Harington's arguments, which survived among his papers.[27] Harington's *Tract* is impressive as a well-reasoned plea for moderation in religious matters and for its cumulative weight of argument in favor of James's claims. The well-tempered rhetorical strategy of convincing each group in turn by quoting from one of their own members is founded on an enthusiastic belief that James is meant by Providence to be king: no wonder, in that case, that statements from all sorts of quarters converge to support his claims. Once "applied," these quotations are revealed as prophecies—witting or unwitting—of the coming of that paragon of earthly virtue, James Stuart. Most impressive of all in the *Tract* is the vision of the embittered Papist, Protestant, and Puritan sectarians of late Elizabethan England reconciled in a dawning Jacobean era of mutual respect and toleration:

. . . of all three there ar men learned, and not onely civillie honest, but heartilie devout . . . howsoever estraunged or divided in other matters of faith, or prone in disputes, yet in this matter of State of all worldlie matters most important wee may all hold together, and who knoweth whether a sound accorde in a matter of so great moment may not be a great inducement to a better agreement in matters of Religion? (5)

A Short View of the State of Ireland

Harington's application for an Irish archbishopric and chancellorship begins by acknowledging the difficulty common to all job applicants, the indignity of having to apply at all. He concludes that it is a necessary evil in an age which is "aptest to thinke better of them that thinke best of themselves" (1).[28] More serious obstacles lie in his scanty legal and theological qualifications for the posts. Harington's answer is that what is needed to bring peace to Ireland is not legal expertise (lawyers have already tried and failed) or military strength (it is in the army's interest to promote quarrels), but a Parliament to settle land claims, followed by the ministrations of a mediator equipped with "an upryght conscyence and generall understanding of the grownds of the laws of God and nature." He has the disposition and dexterity for such work, and has had some success in the past (6–8).

In religious matters, likewise, it is more than anything "myld conferences" showing how reasonable the tenets of the Reformed Church are, and how similar in spirit to Roman Catholicism, that are needed. Harington remarks that it is no wonder that the attempts to convert the Irish to Protestantism over the years have been so unsuccessful, when the Reformers resorted to pulling down crosses and destroying saints' images in the Catholics' churches, abusing their saints and ceremonies in sermons, flouting their holy days, and "pronowncing that all theyr awncestors are damned that did but pray to owr Lady" (19). He gives samples of the kind of preaching he would encourage, on vestments, confession, fast days, and miracles. Where he saw crosses or images remaining in Irish churches in his own time there, he says,

I told them owr Church did not condemne the use but the abuse of thease, when throwgh a neglygent and affected ygnorawnce the peeple creep to them and are prostrate afore them as to deytyes; but for those that wold breake them and defase them . . . I assewred them owr Church held them as worthy of punishment as owr State held theyr cowntryman that trayld Queen Elisabeth's picture at his horse tayle. (16)[29]

Harington has to overcome not only his lack of qualifications but also his reputation for lightheartedness. He protests that his policies for legal reform are not a Utopian dream (6) and anticipates that his readers may at first "smyle at the reeding of this that follows" and think "the example ys strawnge for a Knight, a layman, and one moche conversant in lyght studyes and poetry, to bee made a Byshop and a Preest" (13, 19). His answer here is twofold: that he has now bade farewell to "all poetry and lyght studyes" (11); and that poetry, as a branch of learning, should in any case be no obstacle to high office, as Sidney's example, among others, should prove. Moreover, theology and poetry have a natural affinity, as he has shown in his commentary on Virgil (20).

As for his special fitness for the posts, Harington first cites his advantages of birth, his honorable life, and his two visits to Ireland, "once in the profowndest peace and quyet that ever yt enjoyed in Queen Elisabeth's days, after in the sharpest and moste chargeable war that hath been in that realm since the Crown of England had any interest in yt." On his first visit, he learned much about the theory and practice of colonization and about the Desmond rebellion and the "tragedyes of rapin, flyght, and famin" in Munster; on his second he observed the shortcomings of the English military commanders (2–3). Summing up his case at the end, he stresses the expenses and dangers of his war service in Ireland on this second visit; he offers himself as the king's chaplain in Ireland as he was formerly the queen's champion there (22–23).

Harington's treatment of the Irish problem represents "the liberal Tudor point of view," in Edward M. Hinton's words; David Beers Quinn rightly calls it an "urbane and tolerant" approach.[30] Harington's optimism about how far the sweet reasonableness of the amateur could go in solving Ireland's civil and religious disputes is reflected in his extraordinary sanguineness about his own abilities and prospects. It took an original outlook to protest that he was serious about his suit while adding this engaging mixture of superstition, anecdote, and generous judgment of the Irish:

As for mee I thinke my very *genius* doth in a sort lead mee to that Cowntry: for—whereas dyvers are wont to complayn, some of the dawngerows passages thether, some of an yll affection of that people to owr nacion, some of the soyle and ayr not agreeing with them, some that the Realm in generall ys beggerly and of no account—I thank God I, for my part, have crost that sea fowr severall tymes, in depth of winter, in heat of sommer, yet skarse was sea-sycke; I never fownd in the remote sheers of England or Walls eyther the gentry more kynde in theyr fashion of intertaynment, or the marchawnts and townsmen and women more cyvill in behaveowr, or the mean sort and peasawnts more loving and servisable whear they are honestly vsed, throwgh all the fyve provinces. . . . (9)

Equally, it took an engaging ingenuity to urge that his recent imprisonment and legal battles, and his sickness and family troubles, have added to his qualifications to be lord chancellor and archbishop, by quickening his mind, increasing his knowledge of the law, and mortifying his "vayn and ydle affections" (13).

A Supplie or Addicion to the Catalogue of Bishops

About the middle of 1607, by his own account,[31] Harington began to compile biographical notes on the bishops of the Church of England of his time and of recent memory, as a supplement or "Supplie" to Francis Godwin's *A Catalogue of the Bishops of England* (1601). According to the note Harington appended to the fair copy addressed to Henry Frederick, Prince of Wales, the immediate occasion was this rhyme, then current:

> *Henry the* 8. pulld down Abbeys and Cells
> But *Henry the* 9. shall pull down Bishops and bells.
>   (191)

Aware of the weight that this "trayterous and malitious prediction" might have carried with factions in the Church and among the credulous by its "mixing falshood with probabillities," Harington determined to recommend Godwin's *Catalogue* for the prince's reading, and to add

this supply unto yt of the late times, with as much fidellitie and perspicuitie and as little partiallity as possiblie I could . . . For in reading of both he shall playnly see that christian religion was first planted by Bishops, that it hath beene preserved and continued with Bishops and that it will fall and decay without Bishops. . . . (195)

Harington often acknowledges his particular royal audience in the *Supplie*. His method has been to suppose while he writes that he is "telling a Story, in your highnes presence and hearing" (189). He aims at "a faithfull report" but also "to sawce it in such sort, with some varietie of matter not impertinent, to cheere your spirit, least a dull relation of the acts of grave graybeards to a young prince might grow fastidious" (59). Where Godwin wrote for publication, Harington can be more frank in what he says because he writes "but privately to your highnes" (44).

There are also indications within the *Supplie* that Harington had a wider audience in mind. He says, for instance, that he will not linger too long in discussing the see of Oxford "for I know this discourse is to some as *Unguis in ulcere* [a nail in a wound]" (143). The editor of the *Supplie,* R. H. Miller, comments that the many seventeenth-century manuscript copies in existence "indicate that Harington and his successors were rather free in making texts of the *Supplie* available to others" (2–3).[32]

It was, however, Harington's grandson John Chetwind who first published the *Supplie.* Curiously, it seems then (1653) to have been regarded as an antiepiscopal tract. Chetwind was a Presbyterian and no friend to bishops. He must have decided that there were enough unflattering anecdotes about them in the *Supplie* to suit his Presbyterian tendencies, and the reception of his book seems to have borne him out. Thomas Fuller wrote in *The Worthies of England* that in it "(besides mistakes) some tart reflections *in uxoratos episcopos* [on married bishops] might well have been spared."[33] Anthony À Wood describes the reception of Chetwind's book thus: ". . . no sooner it was published, and came into the hands of many, but 'twas exceedingly clamour'd at by the Loyal and orthodox Clergy, condemning him much that published it . . . it was exceedingly pleasing to the Presbyterians and other Dissenters."[34]

Such a reception was made possible by the fact that Harington is not as forthright in his defense of bishops in the body of the *Supplie* as he was in the note describing its occasion.[35] But there are indications of his views within the *Supplie:* Dr. Bancroft's example prompts the comment that "envy it selfe cannot but gratulate the Church of England that is so furnished with learned Bishops" (40); in the life of Dr. Sands Harington expresses the wish that squires and knights should be "fuller of Reverence toward Bishops, and Archbishops; and not to oppose or contest them" (167–68). More-

over, Harington's attitude toward the Puritans in the Church is in
no doubt. While he takes pleasure, for example, in Bancroft's dis-
comfiting of the Papists (43) his real animus is against the opposing
extreme faction, the "fantasticall Novelists," Puritans best defined
as "Protestants skard out of their witts" (42, 38).

Harington's heroes are those like Dr. Andrewes who bravely re-
sisted pressure from a patron to support Puritan views, and Dr.
Dove, who defended the use of "Rhetoricall figures and tropes, and
other artificiall ornaments of speach taken from prophane authors"
against the Puritans (139–40, 147). The "trew Theorike and Prac-
tick of Puritanisme" is to impugn the authority of bishops in lectures
while impoverishing bishoprics by selling long leases on Church
property (144).

It is the depredation of the institutional wealth of the Church
that is Harington's most persistent complaint in the *Supplie*.[36] It is
not only the bishops who have been guilty. Queen Elizabeth herself
was culpable in despoiling the see of Ely while Heaton was bishop
(90–92). Leicester and his father "made no great conscience to spoyle
the Church lyvings" (182). A kind of judgment on the despoilers
may be seen in the fate of Sir Walter Raleigh, now in the Tower,
who took Sherborne castle, park, and parsonage from the see of
Bath and Wells (101–3); the Dukes of Somerset and Northumber-
land divided the sees of Bath and Durham between them, "like the
soldiers that cast lotts for Christes garment," but were both beheaded
in the Marian restoration (183–84).

Lead and brass from roofs, coffins, and statues have been despoiled,
at Bath and Wells and at Hereford and York (115, 130, 159–60).
Bishop Kitchin of Llandaff, in spite of his name, "in the spoyle of
that see . . . was as little frend to the Kitchen as the rest, spoyling
the woodes and good provisions that should have warmd yt" (155).
Dr. Capon "made a Capon of his bishopprick, and so guelded it,
that it will never be able to build either Church or Castle againe"
(98). Exeter is now "rather worthie of pittie then envy, having but
two Mannors left of 22" (127).

Almost as much scandal, in Harington's eyes, had attached itself
to the Church because of the marriage of bishops. It was noted
earlier how in the *Epigrams* Harington is consistently opposed to
the marriage of the clergy.[37] In the *Supplie,* the examples of unfortunate clerical marriages pile up: Bishop Cooper's wife (though he
married her on the only possible justification, the avoiding of sin)

was notoriously unfaithful (78–79); Bishop Berkeley's wife made him persecute his predecessor's family unjustly and carried off all his money when he died (117); Bishop Elmer's daughter married a minister, one Mr. Adam Squyre, who preached at his own marriage upon the text, *"It is not good for Adam to be alone,"* and so pursued it that "after he had bene some yeares married, that though his wife were away, yet Adam would not be alone" (49).

One of Harington's strengths as a historian is the range of sources he draws on in addition to published histories and the many controversial writings with which he was familiar.[38] The notes on Bishop Overton, for instance, are based on "the generall speach as I have traveld through the Contrie, which is not to be contemned, for *Vox populi, vox dei est*" (96–97); tradition and legends about the founding of Bath are included (106 ff.). He has heard sermons by a great many of the bishops he discusses and has observed the reactions of the congregation: during Bishop Hutton's sermon on the sensitive issue of the succession in the chapel at Whitehall the queen was listening "at the window in the Closet" (170–71). Harington knew some of the figures in his history as a schoolboy at Eton, and at Cambridge; he reports a tale about Bishop Cooper he heard on first coming to court (77), and the changes in the see of Gloucester he has observed on his own travels over the years (58).

Harington's list of his own advantages over Godwin as a historian includes a comment on his privileged sources of information as a courtier: "I livd in the place where I might know many things without enquyrie, which had been skarce safe for him in that tyme to enquyre after" (44). In one case, Harington was able to question the bishop's wife who was the subject of a current piece of scandal— she happened to be a cousin of his wife's—and later historians have accepted his scotching of the story (34–35 and n. 4). Bishop Robinson himself has told Harington about a conversation he had with Queen Elizabeth, so that the account Harington gives is not based "upon meere conjecture" (186–87). On other occasions he is prepared to include anecdotes that may be unreliable, for the sake of the color they add to his account, while he safeguards his integrity as a historian by acknowledging their doubtfulness. He "cannot preciselie affirme" that the bishop in an anecdote he was told was Thomas Young, "but I dare affirme this man was as worthie of it" (160). It was said that Bishop Cooper received a large legacy after

the death of a great lord, "but bicause I have not seene his last
testament, I cannot preciselie affirme yt" (80).

In any case, the atmosphere in which he writes is one wherein
the truth is always doubtful. On the fascinating story of Bishop
Sands's deception by Sir Robert Stapleton—already noted in the
context of Stapleton's grand building project[39]—Harington
comments:

The fame, or rather Infamie, of this matter, speciallie before their con-
viction, was farre and diverslie spread according as the reporters favord or
disfavord either; and the frends of each side had learned their tale so perfect,
that many long time after held the first impression they had receaved,
notwithstanding the censure and sentence in the Starchamber. (166)

The question of partiality raised here comes up frequently in the
Supplie. In the account of Bishop Gardiner, Harington tells how
Gardiner persecuted his own father and mother but adds, "Yet that
I speake not all out of passion I must confess I have heard some as
parcially praise his clemencie, and good conscience, and namely that
he was cause of restoring manie honorable howses overthrown by
King Henry the eight; and in King Edwards minority" (67).

The basis of this aspiration to impartiality is not so much any
modern regard for absolute historical accuracy as a desire to weigh
the praise or blame proper for his subjects. Looking back over what
he has written at one point, Harington's fear is that insufficient
information will lead him "to obscure and omit the good desarts of
some, and to conceale and hide the demerits of others" (126). Where
his subject is a close friend like Bishop Toby Mathew, the twin
problems of impartiality and proper praise and blame are most in
his mind; he begins his account with a rhetorical flourish on the
question:

The praises of a frend are partiall or suspitious, of straungers, uncertaine
and not judicious, of courtly persons complementall and mannerly, of
learned and wisemen more pretious, of a prince most cordiall and comfortable, but of an Adversarie though often daungerous, yet never unde-
served. What exceptions then can be taken to his just praises, whom frends
commend, straungers admire, nobles imbrace, the learned affect and im-
itate his soveraigns have advaunced, and even his enemie and emulous
cannot chuse but extoll and approve. (175)

In his anedotes Harington's historical method and aim to entertain are in the best possible harmony: the story of Bishop Westphaling and the false alarm in Christchurch Cathedral shows the quality of the man vividly, for "Trifling accidents shew as good proofe ofttimes of a mans spirit and courage and constancy as the waightiest occasions" (135). Some of the liveliness, the "sawce" for the "dull relation" of the *Supplie*, comes also from Harington's metaphors. They often give a glimpse of everyday life in his world. On Bishop Andrewes's slow promotion in the Church, he says,

as an industrious merchant that secretlie and diligentlie follows his trade with small shew, till his wealth being grown so great it can be no longer hidden is then calld on for Subsidies and loans and publique services, so did this mans excellency suddenly breake forth. (139)

He comments that "facetious passages" such as Toby Mathew's witticisms are "as delightfull to the hearer as a fair course at tilt is to the beholders, where the staffe breaks both at the poynt and Counterbuffe even to the hand" (178).

Most fully developed is the metaphor of the army and of warfare. The hard beginning and late triumph of the reformed Church of England are likened to a battle in which those in the first assault suffered great losses, but those coming after achieved victory (33). In the present mutiny of the schismatics (mainly the Puritans, presumably), a "Corporall or a gentleman of a band" may prevail better than more senior officers (195); Harington's account of the Church's struggles

must be borne with therein as they that report Battells fought, at which themselves were present, who though they could not from any one place see all the feats of Arms, and defeats that they wryte of, yet telling part of that he saw and felt . . . and gathering part by the sequell, and some by other mens report, or the enemies confession, is supposed to wryte a trew history. (196)

Harington's account of Bishop Godwin illustrates many of the best qualities of the *Supplie*. Godwin came to grief because of an unwise marriage to a London widow; Sir Walter Raleigh, who had long had his eye on a manor in the bishopric, tried to use the queen's disapproval of such matches to further his claims (117). Harington

himself carried Raleigh messages from the queen on the matter; the
bishop became the subject of court gossip and was forced to give
up Wivliscombe Manor to pacify his persecutors (118). Harington
sums up: "he neither gave Willsombe [Wivliscombe] for love, nor
sold yt for money, but left yt for feare." Godwin himself "protested
to me with teares in his eyes" that his marriage was a pure one, he
says, and he concludes with a tribute to his hospitality, learning,
and conduct: "His reading had bene much, his Judgement and
doctrine sownd his government mylde and not violent, his mynde
charitable . . ." (120).

It is Harington's many-sided engagement with Godwin's story—
as a friend, an enemy to Raleigh who demanded the despoiling of
the see, and an opponent of the marriage of the clergy—that enlivens
his account. He is fascinated by the interweaving of his two favorite
themes of clerical marriage and ecclesiastical depredations in Godwin's case, and with the mystery that remains about how he fell,
good man as he was: "How straungly he was intrapt in that unfit
marriadge I know not" (120). The author of a modern history of
the see of Bath and Wells quotes approvingly from this remarkable
sentence on Godwin's bitter fate:

Thus the bishopprick as well as the bishop were punished, who wished
in his hart, he had never taken this preferment, to soyle himself in his
decrepit age, with that stayne that all his life he had abhorred, and to be
made an Instrument of another mans sacriledge, and used like a leaden
Conduite pipe to convay water to others, and drinke nothing but the
dreggs and drosse and rust it self. (118–19)[40]

Harington's work is meant for the ears of a prince, and is enriched
by personal observation, privileged sources and a lively curiosity
about the other powerful figures in its pages. Its author is deeply
engaged in the issues and personalities of his history, yet also imposes
on himself a high standard of impartiality. As a document of church
history it would be hard to match anywhere.

On Marriage

In his *Orlando,* Harington mentions "a litle dialogue of mariage
that I made in my young dayes" (23.A). This is the only evidence
that the work existed.[41] It is mentioned in connection with Harington's interpretation of Astolfo's disarming himself before mount-

ing the hippogriff as an allegory of the necessity of the priest or theologian to "cast away the burdenous clog of all worldly incumbrances and, to use the phrase of our Saviour him selfe (leave father, wife, and children)." This view of marriage as an encumbrance for the man of religion is balanced by a note earlier in Harington's *Orlando* extolling marriage for the rest of mankind, urging them to "concord in matrimonie" and adding, "you shall hardly find a discreet loving husband . . . but is with all the vertuous good minded man, be they of what calling they list" (5.M.).

Late in his career, Harington returned to the topic of marriage in a letter to Bishop Joseph Hall, apparently intended for publication, though a draft in Harington's manuscript papers in the British Library is the only known version of it.[42] In the letter, Harington refers to two works by Hall: his "An Apologeticall discourse of the mariage of Ecclesiasticall persons," published in the first volume of his *Epistles* (1608), a letter addressed to Harington himself, on the question "Whether a man and wife after some yeares mutuall, and loving fruition of each other, may upon consent, whether for secular, or religious causes, vowe and performe a perpetuall separation from each others bed, and absolutely renounce all carnall knowledge of each other for ever," published in the third volume in 1611.[43] This second epistle is apparently in reply to a statement of Harington's on abstinence in marriage (now lost) along the lines of Hall's title. On the marriage of clergy, Harington says in his letter that he has given his opinion against ecclesiastical marriages—that they are "unexpedient," though not unlawful— "in divers of my wrytings," and mentions a number of his epigrams on the subject (82–83).

Harington is an entertaining controversialist. Although he holds "ye flatt contradictory" to Hall's opinions on the marriage of priests and marital abstinence, he does not try to match the earnestness of his opponent; he sustains a lighthearted, combative tone, mixing ironic jibes, telling anecdotes, commonsensical objections, and challenges to Hall's interpretations of his authorities. The courtier in Harington reflects on colorful and powerful personalities he has known; Lord Burghley, who suspected any cause in court defended by an array of noteworthy counsel; King James's public and private opinions; and of course Elizabeth, who did not favor the marriage of ministers and would not allow their children to inherit.

The attitudes underlying Harington's tone in the letter are complicated. He is genially tolerant about, say, adultery, recalling his own joking epigram "to a Lady that was as austere as I was carlese" on the subject (no. 408; 84–85). On the other hand, he supports rules to save the clergy from the fleshliness of marriage. Nor can a moderate conservatism and genial cynicism quite account for Harington's position on the second of the controversies, over marital abstinence. He challenges Hall's account of 1 Corinthians 7, where Paul discusses the topic. Though Harington does not insist that Hall should believe legends about miracles, he clearly thinks the examples of Edward the Confessor (who agreed with his queen to remain virginal and was blessed with a miraculous gift of healing),[44] and that of Joseph and Mary, will command his respect (86). Harington even grows sarcastic:

Wherefore howsoever Mr Hall having a yong and a fair wife may thinke itt a deadlye sinne to defraud her in the Apostles sence [i.e., to practise sexual abstinence], yette the hollye ghoste may (for aught I know) be of another mynde. . . . (85)

As MacKinnon suggests, the dispute is perhaps influenced by the contrast between Harington's own situation, "in his fifties, in failing health, married for nearly thirty years and father of eleven children"—and Hall's, in his thirties and newly married.[45] In this area Harington's views have changed: his preference for abstinence in marriage contrasts with the "discreet loving husband" who wrote the notes to *Orlando*.

Chapter Six
Conclusion

Harington translated the forty-six cantos of *Orlando Furioso* into what he called "English heroical verse," surrounded the translation with essays and annotation, and supervised the production of the lavish illustrated edition in which it was published. He wrote a long, Protean pamphlet that described a modification to the privy, satirized fastidiousness and hypocrisy, and collected a range of entertaining material on the unlikely subjects of excretion and sanitation. He wrote hundreds of epigrams in imitation of Martial, incorporating barbed comments on personalities from the court and the town, traditional lore from the country and incidents from his domestic life. He translated Book 6 of the *Aeneid* and wrote a commentary for Prince Henry on the question of how much true doctrine about heaven and hell a pagan like Virgil could have known. He put all 150 psalms into verse, in a huge variety of meters. He wrote tracts on a controversy about the coming of Elijah, on gambling, on the succession to Queen Elizabeth and the resolution of the religious question, and one on the state of Ireland. He collected notes on the bishops of the English Church, recording all sorts of incidents in their careers and his own lively opinions about them.

In a career full of ambitious and generally disappointing projects, he visited Ireland twice, once as a colonist and again as a soldier. Throughout his career, he divided his time between the court and his estates in Somerset, observing and intriguing in one and building, experimenting, and improving in the other. Late in his life he was involved in quarrels over inheritances and in a disastrous family debt, which put him in prison. He was on familiar terms with the powerful figures of his day, with Queen Elizabeth and King James, with great noblemen, upstart adventurers, and a miscellaneous collection of bishops. Harington is thus one of those men of Renaissance Europe who embraced a range of practical and artistic interests that seems impossibly wide to a more specialized age, even if, when put beside the giants of his group—Sidney or Bacon, let alone Leonardo—he is of course a diminutive figure.

There is no doubt that his writings were well known in his own time. There was a scandalous story attached to the origins of his Ariosto, and the finished work was certainly widely read. It seems generally to have been well received, though there were those who decried it. The *Metamorphosis* produced a crop of "Ajax" puns in Elizabethan writing and a reaction that was divided between distaste for its subject matter and admiration for the witty way it was treated. The epigrams circulated widely in manuscript and their author was established as a leading exponent of the newly fashionable genre.

The lasting influence of these works, in strictly literary terms, is harder to establish. The guise of the fool that Harington took on to "have his tale heard" made it difficult to take what he did seriously. His *Orlando* is perhaps the exception: it was the first complete English translation of Ariosto's poem, and helped it play its part in the Elizabethan vogue of the romance. The first three books of *The Faerie Queene* came out before Harington's translation, so Spenser must have read his *Orlando* in the Italian, but it is likely that Shakespeare used Harington's version for the Hero-Claudio plot in *Much Ado About Nothing,* and echoes of Harington's translation have been heard in *Venus and Adonis* and *The Rape of Lucrece.* Milton, we know, read the poem in Harington's version.[1] The significance of the book itself should not be forgotten, either: its handsome apparatus of engraved illustration and copious commentary was a striking innovation in English book production.

Where he was noticed at all in succeeding centuries, Harington was generally slighted. He was regarded as an unreliable historical source by the biographers and church historians of the seventeenth and eighteenth centuries; in the *Dictionary of National Biography,* of which the appropriate volume came out in 1890, Mandell Creighton concluded Harington's entry by saying, "His translation of the 'Orlando Furioso' has been superseded and his epigrams, disfigured by coarseness, are forgotten."[2] Sir Walter Raleigh's pioneering essay in 1896 took issue with this view and discussed Harington as an important chronicler of his times.[3] Another sympathetic account came from Lytton Strachey, who included Harington among his *Portraits in Miniature* (1931). In his conclusion, Strachey muses on the oblivion into which his subject has passed: the *Orlando* unread, the letters known only to a few historians, the books of epigrams hidden in the depths of libraries, and Englishmen, for all their pride in the English sanitary system, giving never a thought to the inventor of the water closet.[4]

Not much had changed by the 1950s, when C. S. Lewis was writing his volume on the sixteenth century in the *Oxford History of English Literature*. Lewis mentions Harington four times, his works (the Ariosto and the *Metamorphosis*) occupying not much more than a page of Lewis's 550. The translation is treated sympathetically— neither Harington nor Fairfax, who translated Tasso, is a man of genius, but the reader who cannot study Ariosto and Tasso in the original "can get, not all, but a great deal, of their real quality from Harington and Fairfax." Lewis finds elements in Harington's *Orlando* a little "raw and provincial," all the same. The *Metamorphosis* he finds unworthy of its English predecessors in humorous prose: "More had been a grave droll and Nashe a clown; Harington is only a wag."[5]

Since Lewis wrote, a great deal has been done to make Harington's work better known and more accessible. His Ariosto is available in three modern editions and in facsimile. The *Metamorphosis* and the *Supplie* can be read in annotated critical editions; there are modern facsimiles of two editions of *Nugae Antiquae*. Scholarly articles have illuminated biographical, editorial, and critical aspects. Dissertations have advanced our understanding of Harington's epigrams and of his *Orlando*.

From all this, and from a fresh look at Harington's work as a whole, a more rounded picture emerges. Harington can be seen as a significant participant in the culture of his time: active in bringing into it by translation, interpretation, and paraphrase materials from Virgil and the Psalmist, as well as from Ariosto; active in fixing court gossip, folk wisdom, and classical models in the medium of the epigram; active in bringing his version of good sense and tolerance to questions of the day like gambling, the succession to Elizabeth, and the Irish rebellion; and active in church matters, from early indiscretions with Papist books to his mature view of religious toleration and his pleas against the spoiling of the Church and the marriage of clergy. If in this view the *Metamorphosis,* for which he gained lasting notoriety, recedes a little in prominence— its antipuritanical stance clearer, its waggishness more purposeful— then the *Orlando* volume becomes if anything more central, as a compendium of attitudes on current topics and a major effort of interpretation as well as of translation.

A study of Harington's writings provides some unexpected van-
tage points on his period. For instance, scattered comments in his
writings give an idea of how one participant saw the literary scene
around him. Here Sir Philip Sidney looms largest, as both theorist
and practitioner; Spenser figures prominently; lesser poets like Daniel, Constable, and Dyer appear as friends, Raleigh as courtier rather
than poet, and a host of lesser writers are mentioned: fellow-trans-
lators like Phaer, Golding, and Hudson, and fellow-epigrammatists
like Churchyard and Bastard. Bringing up the rear is a shadowy
crew of hacks and poetasters, included in the epigrams under their
own or borrowed names. Harington was clearly familiar with the
theaters of his day and mentions a variety of stage performances,
from the act of the comedian Tarlton through London comedies to
academic dramas. He owned a remarkably comprehensive collection
of published plays. Jonson says Harington asked him what he thought
of his epigrams. Yet we hear almost no echoes of the playwrights
in his writings, almost nothing of Marlowe, Shakespeare, or Jonson
himself, beyond a reference to *The Jew of Malta* in an epigram (no.
214) and a solitary (unsympathetic) reference to Sir John Falstaff in
the notes to *Aeneid* 6. Sir Walter Raleigh's comment in his essay
on Harington was that "had he known but half as many dramatists
as he knew bishops, we should not have been left groping in the
ash-pit for the sorry relics that go to make a history of Elizabethan
literature."[6]

In the area of interpretation Harington's allegorizing proves to
be something different from what the modern prejudice against such
methods might lead us to expect. It does not produce a set of
abstractions remote from the experience of reading, nor does it rely
blindly on authorities. Commenting on *Orlando Furioso*, Harington
applies the poetry to his own world, to the perplexing moral choices
life presented. Like his Virgil volume, his Ariosto is a work of
assimilation; in both, poems from remote civilizations—from sophisticated Renaissance Italy and pagan Augustan Rome—are adjusted and interpreted so that they can be brought to bear on his
own culture.

The religious revolution of his age looks from Harington's stand-
point to be as much a matter of politics as of theology, and though
loyal to the English Church he regarded Roman Catholic practices
less as pernicious superstition than as the Old Faith, shared by all
Englishmen before the Reformation. Its doctrines are thus hallowed

by tradition, and if they are to be discarded, it must be with caution and not with the destructive fervor of the extremists, the iconoclasts, and the persecutors.

A distinctive outlook is apparent in most of the things Harington wrote, difficult to define but nevertheless one of the most interesting aspects of his work. Lewis sums him up as a "wag," suggesting a quality more superficial and more frivolous than true wit. Certainly, the boundaries of good taste and of expected behavior seem often to have provoked a reaction in him in which the temptation to attract attention by self-conscious violation of these limits was mixed with a serious interest in challenging conventional morality. He distrusted self-righteousness and rigid standards of behavior; they are exposed, in the *Metamorphosis* and in countless epigrams, as hypocrisy.

The basis for his attitude is the inescapably imperfect nature of man. According to his outlook, fallible human nature will always assert itself against pretensions to absolute, self-righteous perfection. Far from taking a stern view of those lapses, Harington delights in them, as triumphs of the pleasure principle and of life itself. The reader is involved by his enjoyment of the bawdy passages in Ariosto, the lavatory humor of the *Metamorphosis*, and the satiric deflation of the epigrams. This involvement can be the foundation for a proper understanding of sinfulness: it is an acknowledgment of those baser parts of human nature in which everyone shares. In Jean Humez's phrase, excretion and sexuality are Harington's touchstone of the animal in man. This understanding is the basis for a charitable tolerance, which can distinguish venial sins from truly heinous sins against God and one's fellow-man.

Harington's urbanity has its roots in this outlook: it enables him to adopt a teasingly ironic view about the wantonness of *Orlando Furioso;* to see an essential, natural morality in the *Aeneid* beyond its paganism; to shock his readers into seeing both the analogy and the difference between a stinking privy and a corrupt soul; to puncture self-important and self-righteous atttitudes in the epigrams; to see good men on all sides in the religious controversies and to see a role for rational persuasion even in dealings with the Irish rebels. It is also based in a firm religious piety. Harington's tolerance has its limits; he views the marriage of the clergy as a serious impediment to their spirituality, and the progressive dismemberment of the Church's property as a victory of the selfish greed of the powerful over a proper respect for an institution that represents God on earth. Harington's rational views have their limits, too: however skeptically he scrutinizes historical evidence, he prefers the Scylla of superstition to the Charybdis of an atheism that would doubt everything, and (late in his life at least) invests a special, even a miraculous, power in chastity.

There is much for the modern reader to enjoy in Harington's poetry: passages in *Orlando* in which the narrative moves forward with a confident robustness that is Harington's own, or where his version lingers over a lover's unbearable excitement or pathetic lament, a pious elegy or a meditation on lost things, and epigrams in which experience is neatly or pungently shaped into a satisfying form. Harington's prose retains its vitality; its author is vividly present and his audience rarely forgotten. The writing does not achieve, or even aspire to, that level where traces of an individual personality disappear, the pinnacle of a timeless and seamless eloquence. Harington's style is plain and his art impure: he is at his best when he speaks in a voice authentically his own, and at his worst when he departs from it to strive for mere elaboration or effect.

It is, in fact, just those traces of an individual Elizabethan and Jacobean consciousness and those details of objects and arrangements throughout his work that give it its interest for the modern reader. Harington is in a special sense a marginal figure: taking advantage of the peripheral space of an actual or metaphorical margin to insert a highly personal comment, to come before the reader in his own person.[7] This is literally the case in the *Orlando* volume, of course, where the spaces beside the text of the translated poem, and between sections of it, are filled with a commentary interpreting it in terms of Harington's own experiences and culture—in effect, domesticating Ariosto's poem—and displaying Harington himself, his thoughts, opinions, and *jeux d'esprit*. In the *Metamorphosis,* though there are footnotes that provide the same sort of opportunities, the distinction between text and margin is not so plain. In fact, the apparatus of commentary, apology, and anticipated and answered objections in that work is practically free-standing, and certainly potentially endless. It is by no means clear what the text on which all this is based actually is—it might be the illustrated instructions for constructing Harington's invention, or the satirical comments on individuals and vices, or (most likely) not a text at all but a metaphor—the many-sided metaphor of the reformed privy. The epigram provided another marginal form: a halfway house between anecdote and art, drawing on classical culture and folk wisdom yet homely enough to retain the impress of an individual personality and experience. In these various kinds of marginal commentary, Harington, in contrast to his contemporaries, responded to an oddly modern impulse to write down what he had seen and heard of the personalities and events in the elevated circle in which he was privileged to move, and what he thought of them. The result is a windfall of unusual insights into Elizabethan and Jacobean England.

Harington was attracted, too, by the margins of the civilized values of his day. Unable to rest within the agreed territory of decorous subjects, he returned again and again to its boundaries, not to pass beyond them as an untrammeled free-thinker or heedless blasphemer and libertine, but rather to explore a crucial distinction between venial and cardinal sins, and between conventional morality and true virtue. The tolerant but principled outlook that informs this process is an individual version of Erasmian humanism; in its light, Harington's career can be summed up as a lifelong argument with the puritanical. It represents what he had to say to his contemporaries, to put beside what he contributed to the cultural enterprise of his day by translating and interpreting other men's works. Characteristically, the form he chose was a series of jests, jests that exploited the limits of the fastidiousness and the prudery of his time. In the event, his reputation as a jester largely obscured the serious implications of his work for his contemporaries, and has done so ever since. The cause is partly in his limitations as a writer: his explorations are not based on a profoundly original vision, as (for instance) Rabelais's are, nor does he have the genius for form that More shows in *Utopia*. He created commentaries rather than works of art. Yet the problem he deals with, the relation between the animal parts of man and the rest—the problem of sinful human nature—is an abiding one, as is the subsidiary question of how a civilized society is to discuss these issues. For these reasons Harington's work may not only serve to reveal the past; it may also have something of importance to say to the present day.

Notes and References

Chapter One

1. *A Short View of the State of Ireland* (1605), ed. W. Dunn Macray (Oxford, 1879), pp. 23–24.

2. *Nugae Antiquae,* ed. Henry Harington and Thomas Park (1804; rpt. New York, 1966), 1:240.

3. *The Letters and Epigrams,* ed. Norman Egbert McClure (1930; rpt. New York, 1977), p. 100.

4. For the details of this section, I follow Ruth Hughey's biography of Sir John Harington's father, in her *John Harington of Stepney* (Columbus, Ohio, 1971), pp. 3–81. See also Ian Grimble, *The Harington Family* (London, 1957), chaps. 1 through 4 and 7.

5. *Nugae Antiquae,* 1:184; *Letters and Epigrams,* p. 136.

6. References are to Sir John Harington, trans., *Orlando Furioso,* by Ludovico Ariosto, ed. Robert McNulty (Oxford, 1972). Prefatory matter and appendixes are cited by page number. Harington divided his notes at the end of each book of the poem into "Morall," "Historie," "Allegorie," and "Allusion"; these are cited in the text after the book number as "M," "H," "A," and "An."

7. *A Supplie or Addicion to the Catalogue of Bishops to the Yeare 1608,* ed. R. H. Miller (Potomac, Md., 1979), p. 67.

8. Printed in Ruth Hughey, ed., *The Arundel Harington Manuscript of Tudor Poetry,* 2 vols. (Columbus, Ohio, 1960).

9. *Nugae Antiquae,* 1:184.

10. *Supplie,* p. 67.

11. *A Tract on the Succession to the Crown* (1602), ed. Clemens R. Markham (London, 1880), p. 103.

12. Hughey, *John Harington,* pp. 60, 55. Harington refers to "my noble godfather, William Erle of Pembrooke" in his *Treatise on Playe* (in *Nugae Antiquae,* 1:220). The incident he relates there about Pembroke is on the authority of a servant, which suggests no great intimacy with the earl.

13. Hughey, *John Harington,* pp. 63, 18; John Collinson, *The History and Antiquities of the County of Somerset* (Bath, 1791), 1:128.

14. *Supplie,* pp. 80–81.

15. *A New Discourse of a Stale Subject, Called the Metamorphosis of Ajax,* ed. Elizabeth Story Donno (London, 1962), p. 135.

16. *Supplie,* p. 83.

17. Harington's epigrams are quoted from McClure's edition, *Letters and Epigrams,* and identified in the text by McClure's numbering system.

18. *Nugae Antiquae,* 1:127–28.

19. John and J. A. Venn, *Alumni Cantabrigienses,* pt. 1 (Cambridge, 1922), 2:310.

20. *Supplie,* pp. 120–21, 136, 94; *Short View,* pp. 7–8.

21. *Metamorphosis,* pp. 85–86; *Supplie,* p. 147.

22. *Nugae Antiquae,* 1:131–35.

23. *Metamorphosis,* pp. 85–86; *Letters and Epigrams,* pp. 61–62.

24. *Metamorphosis,* p. 138. The "Bibler" was a student deputed to read a portion of Scripture at dinner.

25. *Metamorphosis,* p. 221.

26. Venn, pt. 1, 2:310; *Letters and Epigrams,* p. 11.

27. *Metamorphosis,* pp. 123, 163–65.

28. Quoted in *Metamorphosis,* ed. Donno, p. 16.

29. Hughey, *John Harington,* p. 79.

30. Ibid., pp. 255n447, 78–79.

31. *Metamorphosis,* pp. 262–63; *Letters and Epigrams,* p. 89; *Short View,* p. 14; *Tract,* pp. 108–9.

32. J. E. Neale, *Elizabeth I and her Parliaments 1584–1601* (London, 1957), pp. 16–18.

33. *Tract,* pp. 36–37, 25, 35.

34. *Letters and Epigrams,* p. 11.

35. Ibid., p. 40.

36. A warrant of July 1586 authorizes Rogers, Harington, and others to take up to one thousand pounds with them to Ireland: *Calendar of the State Papers Relating to Ireland, 1586–88* (London, 1877), p. 113.

37. Constantia Maxwell, ed., *Irish History from Contemporary Sources (1509–1610)* (London, 1923), pp. 241–44.

38. See R. Dunlop, "The Plantation of Munster, 1584–1589," *English Historical Review* 3 (1888):259; David B. Quinn, *Raleigh and the British Empire* (London, 1962), p. 135; *The Cambridge Modern History,* ed. A. W. Ward et al., vol. 3 (Cambridge, 1907), pp. 600–601.

39. Dunlop, "Plantation," p. 267.

40. Historical Manuscripts Commission, *Calendar of the Manuscripts . . . at Hatfield House,* pt. 4 (London, 1892), pp. 472–73.

41. References collected in the index to Hughey, ed., *Arundel Harington Manuscript.*

42. *Nugae Antiquae,* ed. Park, 1:x n. 2; *Metamorphosis,* p. 256.

43. See, for example, the many excerpts in Robert Allot, comp., *Englands Parnassus* (London, 1600).

44. *Letters and Epigrams,* pp. 74, 77, 110, 137. See *Orlando Furioso,* ed. McNulty, pp. 1–1i, for a summary of the revisions in the 1607 edition.

45. *Letters and Epigrams,* p. 15.

46. Noted in B. E. Burton, "Sir John Harington's Translation of Ariosto's *Orlando Furioso*" (B. Litt. diss., Oxford, 1954), p. 173.

47. In *Nugae Antiquae,* 1:191; *Metamorphosis,* p. 88.

48. In *Nugae Antiquae,* 1:191. For the plays mentioned, see E. K. Chambers, *The Elizabethan Stage* (1923; rpt. Oxford, 1951), 2:37 (but see also Alan C. Dessen, "Jonson's 'Knave of Clubs' and 'The Play of the Cards,' " *Modern Language Review* 62 [1967]:584–85), 3:408, 4:373–74, 376–77, 378. Another academic play, the Countess of Pembroke's translation of Robert Garnier's tragedy *Antonius,* is referred to indirectly in the *Metamorphosis* (p. 199).

49. Printed in F. J. Furnivall, "Sir John Harington's Shakespeare Quartos," *Notes and Queries,* 7th ser., 9 (1890):382–83.

50. Chambers, *Elizabethan Stage,* 3:183.

51. Berkshire Record Office, Reading, Trumbull Additional MS 23, p. 48. According to the list of ca. 1610, Harington had quartos of *Henry IV,* parts 1 and 2, and "Henry the fift. Pistol": Furnivall, "Harington's Shakespeare," pp. 382, 383.

52. *Letters and Epigrams,* p. 140, and see McClure's note on p. 410.

53. John Nichols, *The Progresses and Public Processions of Queen Elizabeth* (London, 1823), 2:261 n. 1.

54. Quoted in Francis J. Poynton, *Memoranda, Historical and Genealogical, Relating to the Parish of Kelston* (London, 1878–85), 4:97–98.

55. Illustrated in ibid., facing p. 97; and see p. 98.

56. Collinson, *History,* 1:128.

57. *Regola delli Cinque Ordini* (1563); though there is no record of the use of this book in England in the period: see John Summerson, *Architecture in Britain 1530 to 1830* (London, 1953), p. 25.

58. *Metamorphosis,* p. 56.

59. Collinson, *History,* 1, facing p. 41.

60. Cf. Ludovico Ariosto, *Orlando Furioso,* 42.78–116; quoted here and below from the edition by Lanfranco Caretti (Milan, 1954).

61. Townsend Rich, Letter, *Times Literary Supplement,* 30 May 1936, p. 460; Margaret Trotter, "Harington's Fountain," *Modern Language Notes* 58 (1943):614–16.

62. *Letters and Epigrams,* p. 418.

63. *Letters and Epigrams,* p. 64.

64. Cf. Ariosto, *Orlando Furioso,* 28.33: "che'l palco mal si giunge al muro" ("[that] the woodwork is badly joined to the wall"). Modern translations of Ariosto, here and below, from *Orlando Furioso,* trans. Allan Gilbert, 2 vols. (New York, 1954).

65. *Supplie,* pp. 119, 150.

66. Ibid., pp. 58, 109, 185; *Letters and Epigrams,* pp. 141–42.

67. *Nugae Antiquae*, 1:210; *Supplie*, pp. 163–66.

68. *Supplie*, p. 54.

69. Nichols, *Progresses*, 3:250–51; Poynton, *Memoranda*, 3:5; *Nugae Antiquae*, 1:105.

70. Quotations below from these notes in *Nugae Antiquae*, 1:165–76.

71. Ibid., 1:167.

72. See chapter 4 below.

73. The incident is referred to again in the *Supplie* (pp. 157–58); the writer may be John Bodenham, who compiled *England's Helicon* (1600): *Supplie*, ed. Miller, p. 157n356.

74. William A. Ringler, Jr., ed., *The Poems of Sir Philip Sidney* (Oxford, 1962), pp. 541–42, 563; *Orlando*, 16.M; 11.M, and p. 2. T. G. A. Nelson suggests that Harington, while admiring Sidney's work, was prompted to parody by its "loftier flights": "Sir John Harington as a Critic of Sir Philip Sidney," *Studies in Philology* 67 (1970):41–56. The case is hard to prove conclusively, since it rests on questions of Harington's tone and implied comparisons.

75. *Metamorphosis*, pp. 207, 230.

76. Epigram no. 340; Samuel Daniel, *The Complete Works in Verse and Prose*, ed. A. B. Grosart (1885–96; rpt. New York, 1963), 1:273–76.

77. Sir John Davies, *The Poems*, ed. Robert Krueger (Oxford, 1975), p. 151; *Metamorphosis*, ed. Donno, pp. 106 n. 126, 260 n. 308.

78. *Metamorphosis*, pp. 158, 218.

79. *Letters and Epigrams*, pp. 93, 94.

80. Ibid., p.66.

81. See chapter 3 below.

82. Grimble, *Harington Family*, p. 123.

83. *Nugae Antiquae*, 1:239–40.

84. Ibid., 1:187, 200–203.

85. Ibid., 1:246, 240–41.

86. Ibid., 1:245; *Letters and Epigrams*, p. 107.

87. For the details of the Irish campaign see Richard Bagwell, *Ireland under the Tudors* (1885–1890; rpt. London, 1963), 3:319–46; L. W. Henry, "The Earl of Essex and Ireland, 1599," *Bulletin of the Institute of Historical Research* 32 (1959):1–23; R. H. Miller, "Sir John Harington's Irish Journals," *Studies in Bibliography* 32 (1979):179–86.

88. *Letters and Epigrams*, pp. 73–74.

89. Ibid., p. 72.

90. Ibid., pp. 72–73.

91. Ibid., pp. 76–79.

92. *Nugae Antiquae*, 1:176–77; *Letters and Epigrams*, p. 74.

93. *Letters and Epigrams,* p. 21 n. 5; pp. 108, 79.

94. Henry, "Earl," p. 1. Harington was asked to supply details about the knighthoods Essex had conferred: see Miller, "Harington's Irish Journals," p. 182, and *Letters and Epigrams,* pp. 81–82, 83.

95. *Letters and Epigrams,* pp. 80, 121–22. Harington's journal has not been discovered. He did not write the journal printed in *Nugae Antiquae,* 1:268–93, as "Sir John Harington's Report concerning the Earle of Essex's Journeys into Ireland, from May 10 to July 3, 1599." See T. G. A. Nelson, "Sir John Harington—A Mistaken Attribution," *Notes and Queries,* n.s. 16 (1969):457, and Miller, "Harington's Irish Journals," pp. 180–82.

96. *Letters and Epigrams,* p. 80.

97. Ibid., pp. 85–86; *Nugae Antiquae* 1:312–13; Grimble, *Harington Family,* pp. 136–37.

98. *Nugae Antiquae* 1:178–79.

99. J. Hurstfield, "The Succession Struggle in Late Elizabethan England," in *Elizabethan Government and Society: Essays Presented to Sir John Neale,* ed. S. T. Bindoff et al. (London, 1961), p. 390.

100. *Letters and Epigrams,* pp. 89, 63; *Tract,* p. 74; Epigram no. 264.

101. *Letters and Epigrams,* pp. 90–91.

102. Ibid., pp. 97, 125; *Nugae Antiquae,* 1:180.

103. *Nugae Antiquae,* 1:326. The lantern and the illustrations of the life of Christ appear in watercolor at the end of Folger MS V.a. 249, an autograph MS of Harington's epigrams presented to Prince Henry in 1605. A draft letter of Robert Cecil's, from which other parts are quoted below, says Harington has been accused of "rayling" at the late queen at his dinners, apparently in an attempt to win James's favor (*Letters and Epigrams,* p. 398).

104. *Letters and Epigrams,* p. 99.

105. Ibid., pp. 101, 102; cf. *The Letters of John Chamberlain,* ed. Norman Egbert McClure (Philadelphia, 1939), 1:179.

106. *Letters and Epigrams,* pp. 104–6, 400. Harington's imprisonment seems to have lasted twenty-one weeks, probably from mid-May to mid-October 1603.

107. *Letters and Epigrams,* pp. 397–98.

108. See ibid., p. 399.

109. *Letters and Epigrams,* pp. 109–11.

110. Ibid., pp. 112–18, pp. 399–400. Lady Rogers's will settled her estate on her grandchildren but did not make arrangements for the disposal of the effects in her house at Cannington (Grimble, *Harington Family,* p. 133).

111. "Epistle," Reading MS, unfoliated. A manuscript translation of Book 4 of the *Aeneid,* British Library Additional MS 60283, has been doubtfully attributed to Harington (see Peter Beal, *Index of English Literary Manuscripts,* 1 [1450–1625], pt. 1 [London, 1980], p. 121). However, the translation shows none of Harington's characteristic touches of style, and there is no external evidence to support the attribution.

112. *Letters and Epigrams,* pp. 126, 95–96.

113. Ibid., pp. 118–21.

114. *Letters and Epigrams,* pp. 34–37, 128–31, 140, 405–8, 410.

115. *Nugae Antiquae,* 1:390–97.

116. *Orlando Furioso,* frontispiece (facing title page in McNulty's edition), 41.An, 43.An; *Letters and Epigrams,* pp. 132–34.

117. *Letters and Epigrams,* pp. 135–37, 141–42; British Library Additional MS 27632, fols. 34, 45–45v.

118. *Treatise on Playe,* in *Nugae Antiquae,* 1:189–90; *Supplie,* p. 145; *Letters and Epigrams,* p. 144.

119. *Letters and Epigrams,* pp. 39–40. John went to Eton, and a list survives of the books he took with him on one occasion: see M. H. M. MacKinnon, "School Books Used at Eton College about 1600," *Journal of English and German Philology* 56 (1957):429–33. For his parliamentary career, see *The Diary of John Harington, M.P.: 1646–53,* ed. Margaret F. Stieg (Yeovil, 1977).

Chapter Two

1. See Jakob Schoembs, *Ariosts Orlando Furioso in der englischen Litteratur des Zeitalters der Elisabeth* (Soden, 1898).

2. In *Musica Transalpina, Altus* (1588). See Mary Augusta Scott, "Elizabethan Translations from the Italian: The Titles of Such Works Now First Collected and Arranged, with Annotations," *PMLA* 11 (1896):400–401.

3. For details of the edition of Ariosto used here and below, and of Gilbert's translation, see chap. 1, above, notes 60, 64. Canto and stanza references in this section are to Ariosto's *Orlando.*

4. James J. Yoch, "Architecture as Virtue: The Luminous Palace from Homeric Dream to Stuart Propaganda," *Studies in Philology* 75 (1978):415. See also Judith Lee, "The English Ariosto: The Elizabethan Poet and the Marvelous," *Studies in Philology* 80 (1983):277–99 (this important article came to my attention too late to be fully taken account of here).

5. "Harts ease," like "sage," "time," and "patience" is the name of a plant (either a pansy or a wallflower: see the *Oxford English Dictionary*).

6. Burton, "Harington's Translation," pp.75 ff. See also Town-send Rich, *Harington and Ariosto: A Study in Elizabethan Verse Translation* (New Haven, 1940), pp.71–75.

7. William Stewart Rose, trans., *Orlando Furioso* (London, 1823–31), 1:vi–vii.

8. See p. 12, above.

9. *Ben Jonson*, ed. C. H. Herford and P. and E. Simpson (Oxford, 1925–52), 1:133; Beaumont, Letter, in Geoffrey Chaucer, *The Workes*, ed. Thomas Speght (London, 1598), n.p.

10. E.g., Richard Haydocke, trans., *A Tracte Containing the Artes of Curious Paintinge Carvinge & Buildinge*, by Giovanni Paolo Lomazzo (Oxford, 1598), and for an unacknowledged borrowing, see Franklin B. Williams, Jr., "*Orlando Furioso* and *Rodomonths Infernall*," *Modern Language Notes* 51 (1936):173–75. For Bacon, see his *Advancement of Learning*, in *The Philosophical Works*, ed. John M. Robertson et al (London, 1905), p. 84 and n. 31, and for Burton, see Rich, *Harington and Ariosto*, pp. 197–98.

11. Sir Walter Raleigh, *Some Authors* (Oxford, 1923), p. 148.

12. See A. R. Humphreys, ed., *Much Ado About Nothing* (London, 1981), pp. 6–8; Inge Leimberg, "Zu *Troilus and Cressida* III/3, 145 ff.," *Anglia* 79 (1961):45–49.

13. For earlier translations, see Lucetta J. Teagarden, "Theory and Practice in English Versions of *Orlando Furioso*," *Texas Studies in English* 34 (1955):18–34; for recent verse and prose translations, see Barbara Reynolds, "Ariosto in English: Prose or Verse?," in Aldo Scaglione, ed., *Ariosto 1974 in America* (Ravenna, 1976), pp. 117–34.

14. Teagarden, "Theory," pp. 26–34.

15. Giuseppe Agnelli and Giuseppe Ravegnani, *Annali delle Edizioni Ariostee* (Bologna, 1933), 1:156.

16. Margery Corbett and Ronald Lightbown, *The Comely Frontispiece: The Emblematic Title-Page in England 1550–1660* (London, 1979), p. 43.

17. See Agnelli and Ravegnani, *Annali*, 1:156–57 and *Orlando Furioso*, ed. McNulty, pp. xliii–xlvi.

18. Noted by Simon Cauchi, "The 'Setting Foorth' of Harington's Ariosto," *Studies in Bibliography* 36 (1983):150, 153.

19. Bodleian MS Rawlinson poet. 125. See Kathleen M. Lea, "Harington's *Folly*," in *Elizabethan and Jacobean Studies Presented to Frank Percy Wilson* (Oxford, 1959), pp. 42–58.

20. E. Gordon Duff, "England," in *Early Illustrated Books*, comp. Alfred W. Pollard (London, 1893), p. 248.

21. Puttenham is named in a manuscript note by Harington to his printer. See W. W. Greg, "An Elizabethan Printer and his Copy," in his *Collected Papers*, ed. J. C. Maxwell (Oxford, 1966), pp. 99–100.

22. References to Sidney in the text are to *An Apology for Poetry*, ed. Geoffrey Shepherd (Manchester, 1973).

23. Percy W. Long, "A Detail of Renaissance Criticism," *Modern Language Notes* 15 (1900):42–45; R. Ellrodt, "Sir John Harington and Leone Ebreo," *Modern Language Notes* 65 (1950):109–10.

24. Plutarch, *Moralia*, 36E (trans. Frank Cole Babbit et al. [London, 1949–76], 1:195).

25. Giuseppe Malatesta, *Della Nuova Poesia* (Verona, 1589), pp. 269–80. See Margaret Trotter, Letter, *Times Literary Supplement*, 30 December 1944, p. 631, and John A. Spevack, "Sir John Harington's Theoretical and Practical Criticism: The Sources and Originality of his Apparatus to the *Orlando Furioso*," (Ph.D. diss., Chicago, 1978), pp. 72–77.

26. See Bernard Weinberg, *A History of Literary Criticism in the Italian Renaissance* (Chicago, 1961), 2:954–1073.

27. Fornari and Lavezuola from the 1584 Franceschi edition, and probably Minturno, *L'Arte Poetica* (1563): Spevack, "Harington's . . . Criticism," pp. 77–104.

28. Marvin Theodore Herrick calls Harington's account "absurd": *The Poetics of Aristotle in England* (1930; rpt. New York, 1976), pp. 30–31; Spevack credits Harington with at least "a partial understanding" of Aristotle's theories (p. 103).

29. Harington is following Sidney, *Apology*, p. 101.

30. *The Honour of the Garter*, in *The Life and Minor Works of George Peele*, ed. David H. Horne, vol. 1 (New Haven, 1952), p. 246.

31. See Lea, "Harington's *Folly*," p. 50; and Greg, "Elizabethan Printer and his Copy," pp. 96–98.

32. *The Poetry of Dante*, trans. Douglas Ainslie (1922; rpt. New York, 1971), pp. 18–21.

33. Dodge, "Spenser's Imitations from Ariosto," *PMLA* 12 (1897):163; Rich, *Harington and Ariosto*, pp. vi, 154.

34. See Simon Fornari, *La Spositione . . . Sopra l'Orlando Furioso* (Florence, 1549), 1:181–84. Cauchi points out that the length of the annotations from Book 4 on was generally adjusted to fit the space left on the printed page at the end of the verse (p. 141).

35. Paul J. Alpers, *The Poetry of The Faerie Queene* (Princeton, 1967), p. 187 n. 29.

36. Michael Murrin, *The Allegorical Epic* (Chicago, 1980), pp. 8–25.

37. The above discussion of Harington's allegorizing is indebted to an article on the subject by T. G. A. Nelson forthcoming in *Studies in Philology*, which Mr. Nelson kindly let me read.

38. On the shift in the Renaissance from the allegorical to the mimetic model of poetry, see John M. Steadman, *The Lamb and the Elephant* (San Marino, Calif., 1974), p. 71.

39. Quotations from the Reading MS, Trumbull Additional MS 23. The pagination in the manuscript starts from the beginning of the translation itself, i.e. after the "Epistle." Two successive pages are numbered 73. In the text below, references will not be given for the "Epistle"; Harington's stanza numbers will be given for the translation; and for the notes and commentary, the manuscript numbering system will be followed, with page numbers not given in the manuscript appearing in brackets, and giving the correct page numbers for pages after 73, also in brackets. Mr. Simon Cauchi of Victoria University, Wellington, New Zealand, is currently preparing the Reading manuscript for publication.

40. Quotations and translations from Virgil are from the Loeb edition, trans. H. Rushton Fairclough, rev. ed., vol. 1 (1916; rpt. London, 1978).

41. The seventeenth-century copyist of the MS of Harington's commentary owned by Professor Marcus S. Goldman used this phrase as a subtitle ("The light of Nature in Heathens").

42. Murrin, *Allegorical Epic,* p. 32.

43. In euhemerizing rather than allegorizing the pagan gods Harington is following St. Augustine, who is often cited in the manuscript. See Augustine, *The City of God Against the Pagans,* trans. Eva Matthews Sanford et al. vol. 5 (London, 1965), p. 413 (book 18, chap. 14).

44. D. W. Robertson, Jr., *A Preface to Chaucer* (Princeton, 1963), pp. 337–65.

Chapter Three

1. See *Metamorphosis,* ed. Donno, p. 11.

2. The echo of Philostilpnos's phrase "publik benefit . . . private bashfulnes" (p. 57) in Harington's reply (p. 62) may indicate that Harington had a hand in writing the letter as well.

3. See p. 19, above.

4. Ernest L. Sabine, "Latrines and Cesspools of Medieval London," *Speculum* 9 (1934):313.

5. Lawrence Wright, *Clean and Decent* (London, 1960), pp. 47, 31–32, 52; Sabine, "Latrines," p. 317.

6. Wright, *Clean,* p. 31; Sabine, "Latrines," p. 313.

7. Antonina Vallentin, *Leonardo da Vinci: The Tragic Pursuit of Perfection,* trans. E. W. Dickes (London, 1952), p. 520.

8. Wright, *Clean,* p. 68.

9. Henry E. Sigerist, "An Elizabethan Poet's Contribution to Public Health: Sir John Harington and the Water Closet," *Bulletin of the History of Medicine* 13 (1943):243.

10. Anthony Powell, *John Aubrey and his Friends* (London, 1948), p. 77.

11. Wright, *Clean,* pp. 103, 107, 205.

12. Hugh Plat, *Sundrie new and Artificiall remedies against Famine* (London, 1596), sig. E.

13. Charles Webster, "Alchemical and Paracelsian medicine," in *Health, Medicine and Mortality in the Sixteenth Century,* ed. Webster (Cambridge, 1979), p. 307; J. U. Nef, *The Rise of the British Coal Industry* (London, 1932), 1:247.

14. Hugh Plat, *The Jewell House of Art and Nature* (London, 1594), sigs. B2, B3v–B[4]. See Charles F. Mullett, "Hugh Plat: Elizabethan Virtuoso," *University of Missouri Studies* 21 (1946–47):96–99.

15. Thomas Nashe, *The Works,* ed. Ronald B. McKerrow, F. P. Wilson (Oxford, 1958), 5:195.

16. Ibid., 3:11.

17. *Ulysses upon Ajax* (London, 1596), sigs. A2–A3, [B7]. For another gibe at the translation, see *Ulysses,* sig.[E4v].

18. *Letters and Epigrams,* p. 66, see pp. 19–20, above.

19. *Nugae Antiquae,* 1:240.

20. Though Jean Robertson suggests that Leicester is "the great Beare that caried eight dogges on him when Monsieur was here" (*Metamorphosis,* p. 171): rev. of *Metamorphosis,* ed. Donno, *Review of English Studies,* n.s. 14 (1963):286–87.

21. See nos. 44–46.

22. G. R. Hibbard, *Thomas Nashe: A Critical Introduction* (London, 1962), p. 64.

23. T. G. A. Nelson points out that there is a similar story in *The Alphabet of Tales,* a collection of stories for preachers ("Death, Dung, the Devil, and Worldly Delights: A Metaphysical Conceit in Harington, Donne and Herbert," *Studies in Philology* 76 [1979]:283; *An Alphabet of Tales,* ed. Mary Macleod Banks [London, 1904–5] 1:51).

24. Norman O. Brown, *Life Against Death* (Middletown, Conn., 1959), p. 209.

25. Ibid. Nelson discusses the epigram in the context of the uses of scatology in other poets in "Death, Dung, the Devil, and Worldly Delights," pp. 272–87.

26. T. G. A. Nelson, "Privie Vaults and Privie Faults: Harington's *Metamorphosis of Ajax,*" Proc. of the Twelfth Congress of the Australasian Universities Language and Literature Association, at Perth, 1969 (Perth, 1970), p. 232.

27. Arthur Stanley Pease, "Things Without Honor," *Classical Philology* 21 (1926):28–29, 36–41.

28. Ibid., p. 42.

29. Erasmus, *The Praise of Folly,* trans. and ed. Clarence H. Miller (New Haven, 1979), p. 132. See Acts 2.13, 26.24.

30. Rabelais, *Gargantua and Pantagruel,* trans. Sir Thomas Urquhart and Peter le Motteux ([1653–94] London, 1929), 1:269; *Le Tiers Livre,* ed. M. A. Screech (Geneva, 1964), p. 43.

31. Erasmus, letter to Martin Dorp, in *Praise of Folly,* p. 156.

32. Rabelais, *Gargantua and Pantagruel,* trans. Urquhart and Motteux, 1:3–5; *Gargantua,* ed. Ruth Calder, M. A. Screech (Geneva, 1970), pp. 9–14. The adage, "The Sileni of Alcibiades," had already been the subject of a long section in Erasmus's *Adages:* see Margaret Mann Phillips, *The "Adages" of Erasmus* (Cambridge, 1964), pp. 269–96.

33. *Nugae Antiquae,* 1:239–40.

34. To judge by emendations in the autograph MS used as printer's copy for the *Metamorphosis,* Harington seems to have found the ideal device "to wype withall" (p. 64) in an Italian source; then added a note mentioning Rabelais and changed the text so that he no longer made the inventor an Italian; and finally changed the note to remove all mention of an Italian source. The section on Gargantua's travels (pp. 68–71) has been much added to at a later date (British Library Additional MS 46368, fols. 3v, 9v–10v).

35. Huntington Brown, *Rabelais in English Literature* (Cambridge, Mass., 1933), p. 65.

36. *The Metamorphosis of Ajax,* ed. Peter Warlock and Jack Lindsay (London, 1927), p. xi.

37. M. A. Screech, *Rabelais* (London, 1979), pp. 53–56.

38. Erasmus quotes the Greek proverb, "An ape is still an ape, even if it is dressed up in royal purple," in *Praise of Folly* (p. 29).

39. Brown, *Rabelais in English Literature,* p. 67.

40. Thomas Coryate, *Coryats Crudities* (London, 1611), sig. e2. The Latin is "graveolentibus facetiis."

41. *Ulysses,* sigs. [B8], [D4v].

42. *Nugae Antiguae,* 1:240.

43. Joseph Hall, *Virgidemiarum* (1597–98), in *The Collected Poems,* ed. Arnold Davenport (Liverpool, 1949), p. 92.

44. Nashe, *Works,* 3:177–78.

45. John Taylor, *The Praise of Hemp-Seed* (London, 1620), sig. Bv.

46. John Marston, *The Poems,* ed. Arnold Davenport (Liverpool, 1961), p. 171.

47. E.g., T[homas] B[astard], *Chrestoleros* (London, 1598), p. 124; Tommaso Garzoni, *The Hospitall of Incurable Fooles,* trans. Edward Blount

(London, 1600), pp. 6, 7; John Cotgrave, comp., *The English Treasury of Wit and Language* (London, 1655), p. 16.

48. On suggested connections between Jacques and Harington, see E. K. Chambers, *William Shakespeare: A Study of Facts and Problems* (Oxford, 1930), 1:404, and Oscar James Campbell, *Shakespeare's Satire* (New York, 1943), p. 55. Quotations from Shakespeare, here and below, are from *The Complete Works,* ed. Peter Alexander (London, 1978).

49. "*Ioh. Harringtoni Hercules, sive de modo quo evacuabatur à faecibus Arca Noae*": *The Courtier's Library,* ed. Evelyn Mary Simpson, trans. Percy Simpson (London, 1930), pp. 45, 32.

50. (4.v. 201–2). Quotations from Jonson's works here and below from *The Complete Plays of Ben Jonson,* ed. G. A. Wilkes, 4 vols. (Oxford, 1981–82).

51. *Letters and Epigrams,* p. v.

Chapter Four

1. Sir John Stradling, *Epigrammatum Libri Quatuor* (London, 1607), p. 82 (translation of Harington's no. 21). McClure prints 428 of Harington's epigrams; there are four more in Folger MS V.a. 249, a collection Harington presented to Prince Henry in 1605.

2. Charles Fitz–Geffrey, *Affaniae* (Oxford, 1601), p. 120; for other commendations, see Stradling, *Epigrammatum,* pp. 32–33, John Owen, *Epigrammatum* (London, 1607), Book 2, nos. 5, 34.

3. Beal, *Index,* pp. 138–41, 628; pp. 131–33; and see Beal's introduction, p. 124.

4. Edward Guilpin, *Skialethia* (London, 1598), sig. Cv.

5. Hall, *Virgidemiarum,* in *The Collected Poems,* pp. 93–94; Guilpin, *Skialethia,* sig. [B8].

6. Hoyt Hopewell Hudson, *The Epigram in the English Renaissance* (Princeton, 1947), pp. 8–16.

7. George Puttenham, *The Arte of English Poesie* (1589), ed. Gladys Doidge Willcock and Alice Walker (Cambridge, 1936), p. 54.

8. J. W. Mackail, ed., *Select Epigrams from the Greek Anthology* (London, 1911), p. 4.

9. Otto Seel, "Ansatz zu einer Martial–Interpretation," in Gerhard Pfohl, ed., *Das Epigramm: Zur Geschichte einer Inschriftlichen und Literarischen Gattung* (Darmstadt, 1969), p. 162; T. K. Whipple, *Martial and the English Epigram from Sir Thomas Wyatt to Ben Jonson* (Berkeley, 1925), p. 301.

10. Quotations and translations are from the Loeb edition, *Epigrams,* trans. Walter C. A. Ker, 2 vols. (London, 1968); references to epigrams by book and number are given in the text.

11. See the notes in *Letters and Epigrams;* Jean McMahon Humez, "The Manners of Epigram: A Study of the Epigram Volumes of Martial, Harington, and Jonson," (Ph.D. diss., Yale, 1971), p. 133.

12. Thomas More, *The Latin Epigrams,* ed. and trans. Leicester Bradner and Charles Arthur Lynch (Chicago, 1953), nos. 190, 140.

13. John Heywood, *"Works" and Miscellaneous Short Poems,* ed. Burton A. Milligan (1956; rpt. Westport, Conn., 1980), p. 224.

14. Heywood, *"Works,"* pp. 93, 53. On Heywood's continuing popularity and influence in the sixteenth and seventeenth centuries, see Whipple, *Martial,* pp. 363–64, 380–81, and Milligan's introduction to the *"Works,"* pp. 2–8.

15. Humez, "Manners," pp. 256–57.

16. M. H. M. MacKinnon, "Sir John Harington and Bishop Hall," *Philological Quarterly* 37 (1958):82.

17. Humez, "Manners," pp. 227–29.

18. Gotthold Ephraim Lessing, *Über das Epigramm,* in his *Gesammelte Werke,* vol 7 (Berlin, 1956), p. 14.

19. *Letters and Epigrams,* p. 421.

20. An English version was published separately, *Bellum Erasmi, translated into englyshe* (London, 1533). For a modern translation, see Phillips, *The "Adages" of Erasmus,* pp. 308–53.

21. Lodge, *A fig for Momus* (London, 1595), sig. A3v; Bastard, *Chrestoleros,* p. 171; Davies, *Poems,* p. 129.

22. Davenport, ed., *The Collected Poems,* by Joseph Hall, pp. lix–lx.

23. Humez, "Manners," pp. 167–75.

24. *Letters and Epigrams,* p. 51.

25. G. C. Moore Smith, Letter, *Times Literary Supplement,* 10 March 1927, p. 160; *Metamorphosis,* ed. Donno, p. 232 n. 150; Carolyn J. Bishop, "Raleigh satirized by Harington and Davies," *Review of English Studies,* n.s. 23 (1972):52–56.

26. *Letters and Epigrams,* p. 51.

27. Folger MS V.a. 249, book 1, no. 3 (p. 3).

28. Robert Lacey, *Sir Walter Ralegh* (London, 1973), pp. 90–91, 314, 377.

29. Brownists were followers of the Puritan separatist Robert Browne (ca. 1550–1633), and the Family of Love were mystic pantheists, followers of Henry Nicholas (ca. 1502–ca. 1580). See F. L. Cross and E. A. Livingstone, eds., *The Oxford Dictionary of the Christian Church* (London, 1974), pp. 204, 502, 973.

30. See nos. 159, 75, 418, 104, 241.

31. See nos. 20, 23, 117, 249.

32. See nos. 24, 116, 167, 288.

33. *Nugae Antiquae,* 1:xxiii n.6.

34. "Epigrams of an Elizabethan Courtier," rev. of McClure's 1926 edition of the epigrams, *Times Literary Supplement,* 17 February 1927, p. 104 (extracts of the review were reprinted in *Times Literary Supplement,* 18 February 1977, p. 182).

35. See Whipple, *Martial,* pp. 344–49; *Letters and Epigrams,* pp. 52–53; Oscar James Campbell, *Comicall Satyre and Shakespeare's "Troilus and Cressida"* (San Marino, Calif., 1938), pp. 37–39; Louis Lecocq, *La Satire en Angleterre de 1588 à 1603* (Paris, 1969), p. 228.

36. *Ben Jonson,* ed. Herford and Simpson, 1:133. See J. V. Cunningham, "Lyric Style in the 1590's," in his *Collected Essays* (Chicago, 1976), p. 321.

Chapter Five

1. Francis R. Packard and Fielding H. Garrison, ed., *The School of Salernum: Regimen Sanitatis Salernitanum,* trans. Sir John Harington (1920; rpt. New York, 1970), pp. 11–40, 57–62.

2. Quotations and references in the text below from the Packard and Garrison edition.

3. Packard and Garrison, ed., *School,* p. 31.

4. *Regimen Sanitatis Salerni,* trans. Philemon Holland and Thomas Paynell (London, 1620), p. 3.

5. See Morris Palmer Tilley, *A Dictionary of the Proverbs in England in the Sixteenth and Seventeenth Centuries* (Ann Arbor, 1950), p. 162.

6. Robert Burton, *The Anatomy of Melancholy,* 2.2.6.4 (ed. Holbrook Jackson [London, 1932], 2:119).

7. See Hallett Smith, "English Metrical Psalms in the Sixteenth Century and their Literary Significance," *Huntington Library Quarterly* 9 (1946):249–71; Coburn Freer, *Music for a King: George Herbert's Style and the Metrical Psalms* (Baltimore, 1972), pp. 14–49; and Barbara K. Lewalski, *Protestant Poetics and the Seventeenth-Century Religious Lyric* (Princeton, 1979), pp. 39–53.

8. Karl E. Schmutzler, "Harington's Metrical Paraphrases of the Seven Penitential Psalms: Three Manuscript Versions," *Papers of the Bibliographical Society of America* 53 (1959):241 n. 7, cites a note in Harington's papers mentioning two copies of the psalter. See also Epigram no. 398 and *Letters and Epigrams,* p. 87.

9. See Waldo Selden Pratt, *The Music of the French Psalter of 1562* (1939; rpt. New York, 1966).

10. The Old Version was first available in full in 1562, and went through scores of editions thereafter. See Freer, *Music,* pp. 59–72, and Ringler, *Poems of Sidney,* p. 507.

11. *A Short View*, p. 14. In Psalm 22, for instance, Harington prefers the Geneva's "derision" and "nere" to the Prayer Book psalter's "scorne" and "harde at hand" (verses 7 and 11); and prefers the Prayer Book psalter's "gummes" and "my derling" to the Geneva's "jawes" and "my desolate *soule*" (verses 15 and 20). Here and below quotations are from *The Psalter: or Psalmes of David, after the translation of the great Bible: Pointed as it shall be soong in Churches* (London, 1580) and *The Geneva Bible: A facsimile of the 1560 Edition,* ed. Lloyd E. Berry (Madison, 1969). For the Sidneys' sources, see Ringler, *Poems of Sidney,* pp. 505–7, and J. C. A. Rathmell, ed., *The Psalms of Sir Philip Sidney and the Countess of Pembroke* (New York, 1963), pp. xix–xxi. Quotations from the Sidneys' psalter below are from this edition.

12. See C. S. Lewis, *Reflections on the Psalms* (London, 1958), pp. 3–5.

13. None of the words or phrases listed appears in the Prayer Book psalter or Geneva versions of the relevant passages.

14. Rathmell, ed., *The Psalms,* p. xx.

15. *Letters and Epigrams,* p. 144.

16. Aharon Wiener, *The Prophet Elijah in the Development of Judaism* (London, 1978), p. 146.

17. Ibid., p. 149. The question did arise at James's Hampton Court Conference in 1604, however. See Thomas Fuller, *The Church History of Britain,* ed. J. S. Brewer (Oxford, 1845), 5:290.

18. The *Discowrse* is quoted here from *Nugae Antiquae,* 2:281–304.

19. For an account of the Reformation reaction against allegorizing the Bible, and the modified typology espoused by Reformers like Luther and Calvin, see Lewalski, *Protestant,* pp. 111–29. Harington seems here to be allowing a multiplicity of meanings in the Scriptures in medieval fashion, rather than following the Protestants' idea (described by Lewalski) of a typological meaning not separate from the literal but perfecting it, as its symbolic dimension.

20. Quotations from *Nugae Antiquae,* 1:186–232.

21. J. Hurstfield, "Succession Struggle in Late Elizabethan England," pp. 371–72, and J. E. Neale, "Peter Wentworth," *English Historical Review* 39 (1924):182–202.

22. Quotations and references are from Clemens R. Markham's edition of the *Tract.*

23. Apparently translated from the Latin version, *Epistola exhortatoria . . . ad Nobilitatem ac plebem . . . Regni Scotiae* (London, 1548). See M. L. Bush, *The Government Policy of Protector Somerset* (London, 1975), pp. 22, 27, and A. F. Pollard, *England under Protector Somerset: An Essay* (1900; rpt. New York, 1966), pp. 163–65.

24. *A Discourse containing the Author's Opinion of the true and lawful Successor to her Majesty.* It was printed with Wentworth's *Pithie Exhortation* in 1598, after Wentworth's death in the Tower in 1597. See Neale, *Elizabeth I,* pp. 262–63.

25. See T. G. A. Nelson, "Sir John Harington and Henry Constable," *Recusant History* 9 (1967–68):263–64.

26. Hurstfield, "Succession," pp. 369–96.

27. Beal, *Index,* p. 155.

28. Quotations from *A Short View of the State of Ireland,* ed. Macray; references given in the text.

29. This was Sir Brian O'Rourke, who was hanged for his disrespectful treatment of a picture of Elizabeth in 1591: see Bagwell, *Ireland,* 3:213–17.

30. Edward M. Hinton, *Ireland through Tudor Eyes* (Philadelphia, 1935), p. 71; David Beers Quinn, *The Elizabethans and the Irish* (Washington, D.C., 1966), p. 90.

31. *Supplie,* ed. Miller, p. 191. Miller discusses other evidence bearing out this date on pp. 5–7. Quotations and references below will be to this edition, page numbers given in the text.

32. See also R. H. Miller, "Harington's *Supplie or Addicion to the Catalogue of Bishops:* An Additional Manuscript," *Studies in Bibliography* 35 (1982):171–72.

33. Thomas Fuller, *The Worthies of England* (1662), ed. John Freeman (London, 1952), p. 500.

34. Anthony À Wood, *Athenae Oxonienses* (London, 1691–92), 1, col. 497.

35. In a section he left out of the fair copy presented to Prince Henry, Harington gives a systematic defense of the role of bishops in the Church. This section is printed in Miller, "Sir John Harington's *A Supplie or Addicion to the Catalogue of Bishops, to the Yeare 1608:* Composition and Text," *Studies in Bibliography* 30 (1977):158–61.

36. For an account of these depredations, see Christopher Hill, *Economic Problems of the Church: From Archbishop Whitgift to the Long Parliament* (Oxford, 1956), pp. 14–38.

37. Pp. 92–93, above.

38. See *Supplie,* ed. Miller, pp. 16–19.

39. Pp. 16–17, above.

40. Phyllis M. Hembry, *The Bishops of Bath and Wells, 1540–1640: Social and Economic Problems* (London, 1967), p. 181; on Harington as an unreliable source, pp. 102–3, 156–57. See Miller, *Supplie,* pp. 10–11 and n. 20 on Harington's fate among the historians (mainly, to be quoted but criticized as unreliable). E. Edwards denies hotly Harington's story that Raleigh used Godwin's marriage for his own advantage in *The Life of*

Sir Walter Ralegh (London, 1868), 1:131. J. E. Neale discusses the reliability of an anecdote in the *Supplie* in "The Sayings of Queen Elizabeth" in *Essays in Elizabethan History* (London, 1958), pp. 100–101, leaving the question unresolved.

41. Beal, *Index,* p. 122.

42. Discovered and printed by M. H. M. MacKinnon, "Sir John Harington and Bishop Hall," *Philological Quarterly* 37 (1958):80–86. Quotations and references below are to this version, page numbers given in the text.

43. Hall, *Epistles* vol. 1 (London, 1608), pp. 119–36; vol. 3 (London, 1611), pp. 101–13.

44. On the supposed chastity and miraculous powers of St. Edward the Confessor (King of England 1042–1066), see Frank Barlow, *Edward the Confessor* (London, 1979), pp. 81–85, 259–65.

45. MacKinnon, "Sir John Harington," p. 81.

Chapter Six

1. William Riley Parker, *Milton: A Biography* (Oxford, 1968), 2:849 n. 46, 884 n. 66.

2. *Dictionary of National Biography* vol. 24 (London, 1890), p. 388.

3. Reprinted in Raleigh, *Some Authors,* pp. 136–55.

4. Lytton Strachey, *Portraits in Miniature and Other Essays* (London, 1931), p. 10.

5. C. S. Lewis, *English Literature in the Sixteenth Century Excluding Drama* (1954; rpt. Oxford, 1973), pp. 322 n. 1, 417, 430, 521–22.

6. Raleigh, *Some Authors,* p. 155.

7. See Lawrence Lipking, "The Marginal Gloss," *Critical Inquiry* 3 (1977):609–55.

Selected Bibliography

PRIMARY SOURCES

Main editions of Harington's works, grouped in chronological order of composition.

A Discourse shewing that Elyas must personally come before the Day of Judgement (ca. 1590). In *Nugae Antiquae*. Edited by Henry Harington and Thomas Park. London: Vernor and Hood, 1804, vol. 2, pp. 281–304. Also appeared in earlier editions of *Nugae Antiquae*.

Orlando Furioso in English Heroical Verse. Translated from the Italian of Ludovico Ariosto. London, 1591; rev. ed. London, 1607; rev. ed., "with the Addition of the Authors Epigrams," London, 1634.

Orlando Furioso: Sir John Harington's Translation. Edited by Graham Hough. London: Centaur Press, 1962.

Ariosto's "Orlando Furioso." Translated by Sir John Harington. Selected and edited by Rudolf Gottfried. Bloomington and London: Indiana University Press, 1963.

Ludovico Ariosto's "Orlando Furioso." Translated by Sir John Harington. Edited by Robert McNulty. Oxford: Oxford University Press, 1972.

A New Discourse of a Stale Subject, Called the Metamorphosis of Ajax. London, 1596.

The Metamorphosis of Ajax, A Cloacinean Satire . . . To which is added Ulysses upon Ajax. Edited by S. W. Singer. Chiswick: C. Whittingham, 1814.

The Metamorphosis of Ajax. Edited by Peter Warlock and Jack Lindsay. London: Fanfrolico Press, 1927.

A New Discourse of a Stale Subject, called the Metamorphosis of Ajax. Edited by Elizabeth Story Donno. London: Routledge & Kegan Paul, 1962.

A Treatise on Playe (ca. 1597). In *Nugae Antiquae*. Edited by Henry Harington and Thomas Park. London: Vernor and Hood, 1804, vol. 1, pp. 186–232. Also appeared in earlier editions of *Nugae Antiquae*.

Alcilia. Philoparthens loving Folly. Whereunto is added . . . Epigrammes by Sir J. H. and Others. London, 1613.

Epigrams both Pleasant and Serious. London, 1615.

The Most Elegant and Witty Epigrams. London, 1618; printed with *Orlando Furioso*, 1634.

The Epigrams of Sir John Harington. Edited by Norman Egbert McClure. Philadelphia: University of Philadelphia Press, 1926.

The Letters and Epigrams: Together with "The Prayse of Private Life." Edited by Norman Egbert McClure. 1930. Reprint. New York: Octagon Books, 1977. *The Prayse of Private Life* is almost certainly not by Harington.

A Tract on the Succession to the Crown (1602). Edited by Clemens R. Markham. 1880. Reprint. New York: Burt Franklin, 1969.

MS translation and commentary on Virgil, *Aeneid,* Book 6. Autograph fair copy. Berkshire Record Office. Trumbull Additional MS 23.

A Short View of the State of Ireland (1605). Edited by William Dunn Macray. Anecdota Bodleiana, 1. Oxford: Oxford University Press, 1879.

The Englishmans Docter. Or, the Schoole of Salerne. [Translated from the Latin *Regimen Sanitatis Salernitanum.*] London, 1607. Other editions 1608, 1609, 1617, and 1624.

The School of Salernum: Regimen Sanitatis Salernitanum. Edited by Francis R. Packard and Fielding H. Garrison. 1920. Reprint. New York: Kelley, 1970.

The School of Salernum: Regimen Sanitatis Salerni. Rome: Edizioni Saturnia, 1953.

A Briefe View of the State of the Church of England (1608). Edited by John Chetwind. London, 1653.

A Supplie or Addicion to the Catalogue of Bishops to the Yeare 1608. Edited by R. H. Miller. Studia Humanitas, Catholic University of America. Potomac, Md.: José Porrúa Turanzas, 1979.

MS metrical paraphrase of the complete Book of Psalms. Early seventeenth-century copy. Bodleian, MS Douce 361.

Nugae Antiquae. [Miscellaneous items from the Harington papers.] Edited by Henry Harington. 2 vols. London, 1769–75.

———. Edited by Henry Harington. 3 vols. London, 1779.

———. Edited by Henry Harington and Thomas Park. 2 vols. London, 1804.

SECONDARY SOURCES

Unpublished material is excluded.

Bartley, J. O. "Harington and Saint Basil." *Modern Language Review* 42 (1947):233–34. In his "Briefe Apologie," Harington borrowed from a commentary by St. Basil on reading for the young.

Beal, Peter, comp. *Index of English Literary Manuscripts.* Vol. 1, 1450–1625, part 1. London: Mansell, 1980. Comprehensive listing of

Harington manuscript material, with an introduction also discussing doubtful and lost works.

Bishop, Carolyn J. "Raleigh Satirized by Harington and Davies." *Review of English Studies,* n.s. 23 (1972):52–56.

Brown, Huntington. *Rabelais in English Literature.* Cambridge, Mass.: Harvard University Press, 1933. The *Metamorphosis* as a pioneer English Rabelaisian work.

Cauchi, Simon. "The 'Setting Foorth' of Harington's Ariosto." *Studies in Bibliography* 36 (1983):137–68. Study of the evidence the *Orlando* volume provides of Harington's intentions as a book designer.

Cutts, J. P. "Harington's Epigrammatic Lyric." *Notes and Queries,* n.s. 7 (1960):60–61. Epigram no. 201 written out as a song in three seventeenth-century MSS.

Eliot, T. S. "Epigrams of an Elizabethan Courtier." Unsigned review of *The Epigrams of Sir John Harington.* Edited by Norman Egbert McClure. *Times Literary Supplement,* 17 February 1927, p. 104. Reprint (in part). *Times Literary Supplement,* 18 February 1977, p. 182.

Ellrodt, Robert. "Sir John Harington and Leone Ebreo." *Modern Language Notes* 65 (1950):109–10. Unwittingly repeats Long's discovery of Harington's indebtedness to Ebreo.

Farmer, Norman K., Jr. "A Newly Discovered Holograph Poem by Sir John Harington." *Library Chronicle of the University of Texas at Austin,* n.s. 11 (1979):93–96. Reproduces holograph of Epigram no. 45, from a large-paper copy of the *Metamorphosis* inscribed to Thomas Markham.

Furnivall, F. J. "Sir John Harington's Shakespeare Quartos." *Notes and Queries,* 7th ser., no. 9 (1890):382–83. Transcribes list of plays in Harington's collection from around 1610.

Gaskell, Philip. *From Writer to Reader: Studies in Editorial Method.* Oxford: Oxford University Press, 1978. Discusses manuscripts and editions of Harington's *Orlando Furioso,* and McNulty's edition in particular as a solution to the problems they present.

Gilbert, Allan H. "Sir John Harington's Pen Name." *Modern Language Notes* 58 (1943):616–17. Gives etymology for "Misacmos," Harington's pen name in the *Metamorphosis.*

———. "Nevizanus, Ariosto, Florio, Harington and Drummond." *Modern Language Notes* 62 (1947):129–30. Gives source for Epigram no. 16, and later uses of the source.

Goldman, Marcus Selden. "Sidney and Harington as Opponents of Superstition." *Journal of English and German Philology* 54 (1955):526–48. Discusses references to witchcraft and superstition in Harington's works.

Greg, W. W. "An Elizabethan Printer and His Copy." *Library*, 4th ser., no. 4 (1923):102–18. Reprinted in his *Collected Papers*. Edited by J. C. Maxwell. Oxford: Oxford University Press, 1966, pp. 94–109. On British Library Additional MS 18920, and its use by the printer Richard Field as copy for Harington's *Orlando*.

————. Letter. *Times Literary Supplement*, 12 January 1928, p. 28. Argues that British Library Additional MS 12049—which McClure used for his edition of the epigrams—was not itself a presentation copy, but the manuscript from which the presentation copy for Prince Henry was transcribed.

Grimble, Ian. *The Harington Family*. London: Cape, 1957. Extended treatment of Harington and other Haringtons, making some use of manuscript material.

Harlow, V. T. "Harington's Epigrams." Letter. *Times Literary Supplement*, 14 July 1927, p. 488. On Harington's changing relationship with Raleigh.

Hudson, Hoyt Hopewell. *The Epigram in the English Renaissance*. 1947. Reprint. New York: Octagon Books, 1966. Treats Harington's epigrams as imitations of Martial and pioneers in the vogue of the epigram.

Hughey, Ruth. "The Harington Manuscript at Arundel Castle and Related Documents." *Library*, 4th ser., no. 15 (1934–35):388–444. Introduction to the corpus of Harington manuscripts, at Arundel Castle and elsewhere.

————. *The Arundel Harington Manuscript of Tudor Poetry*. 2 vols. Columbus: Ohio State University Press, 1960. Publishes the Arundel Harington manuscript, a large verse miscellany begun by Harington's father and continued by Sir John himself, with extensive notes.

————. *John Harington of Stepney: Tudor Gentleman: His Life and Works*. Columbus: Ohio State University Press, 1971. Full biography of Harington's father, much authoritative detail on life of Harington himself.

Lea, Kathleen M. "Harington's *Folly*." In *Elizabethan and Jacobean Studies Presented to Frank Percy Wilson*. Oxford: Oxford University Press, 1959, pp. 42–58. Discusses the evidence in Bodleian MS Rawlinson poet. 125 of Harington's revisions of his translation of Orlando and his preparation of it for publication.

Lee, Judith. "The English Ariosto: The Elizabethan Poet and the Marvelous." *Studies in Philology* 80 (1983):277–99. Argues that Harington's translation places the magical and fabulous parts of *Orlando* in a rationalistic and moralistic framework, as an adjustment to the specific demands of its English audience. Rejects claims about Har-

ington's incompetence in favor of the view that he adopts a consistent
strategy as translator and commentator.

Leimberg, Inge. "Zu *Troilus and Cressida* III/3, 145 ff." *Anglia* 79
(1961):45–49. Harington's *Orlando* as a source for an image in *Troilus*,
probably via *The Return from Parnassus*.

Long, Percy W. "A Detail of Renaissance Criticism." *Modern Language
Notes* 15 (1900):42–45. Source for Harington's allegory of the Perseus
myth in the "Briefe Apologie" in Leone Ebreo.

McClure, Norman Egbert. Letter. *Times Literary Supplement,* 19 May 1927,
p. 355. Identifications of pseudonyms in the epigrams.

MacKinnon, M. H. M. "Sir John Harington and Bishop Hall." *Philological
Quarterly* 37 (1958):80–86. Prints draft letter from Harington to
Hall on the marriage of the clergy and marital abstinence.

Miller, R. H. "Sir John Harington's *A Supplie or Addicion to the Catalogue
of Bishops, to the Yeare 1608:* Composition and Text." *Studies in Bibliography* 30 (1977):145–61.

———. "Sir John Harington's Irish Journals." *Studies in Bibliography* 32
(1979):179–86. Corrects errors in previous accounts of Harington's
service in Ireland in 1599, and of his lost journal of the expedition,
by reference to manuscript materials.

———. "Harington's *Supplie or Addicion to the Catalogue of Bishops:* An
Additional Manuscript." *Studies in Bibliography* 35 (1982):171–72.

Moore Smith, G. C. Letter. *Times Literary Supplement,* 10 March 1927, p.
160. Identifies "Paulus" in the epigrams as Raleigh and discusses
some other identifications.

Nelson, T. G. A. "Harington and Dante." *Notes and Queries,* n.s. 16
(1969):456–57. Suggests Harington had probably not read Dante,
despite the references to the Italian poet in the notes to *Orlando.*

———. "Sir John Harington—A Mistaken Attribution." *Notes and Queries,* n.s. 16 (1969):457. Shows that the journal of the Irish campaign
printed in *Nugae Antiquae* is not by Harington.

———. "Privie Vaults and Privie Faults: Harington's *Metamorphosis of
Ajax.*" Proc. of the Twelfth Congress of the Australasian Universities
Language and Literature Association. 5–11 February 1969. Perth:
AULLA, 1970.

———. "Sir John Harington as a critic of Sir Philip Sidney." *Studies in
Philology* 67 (1970):41–56. Suggests Harington's enthusiasm for Sidney's work was tempered by convictions (covertly expressed) about
its limitations.

———. "Death, Dung, the Devil, and Worldly Delights: A Metaphysical
Conceit in Harington, Donne, and Herbert." *Studies in Philology* 76
(1979):272–87. Discusses connections between Harington's use of

scatological imagery in a religious context in Epigram no. 49 (first published in the *Metamorphosis*) and poems by Donne and Herbert.

Raleigh, Walter. "Sir John Harington." *New Review* 15 (1896):277–91. Reprinted in his *Some Authors: A Collection of Literary Essays 1896–1916*. Oxford: Oxford University Press, 1923, pp. 136–55. Reevaluation of Harington's achievement as writer and chronicler of his times.

Rehfeld, Günther. *Sir John Harington, ein Nachahmer Rabelais'*. Halle: Hohmann, 1914. Discusses Rabelais as model for Harington in the *Metamorphosis*, especially for its combination of humanist and folkculture elements.

Rich, Townsend. "Harington's Fountain." Letter. *Times Literary Supplement*, 30 May 1936, p. 460. Suggests Harington built the fountain at Kelston on the lines of the fountain in *Orlando*, Book 42.

———. *Harington and Ariosto: A Study in Elizabethan Verse Translation*. New Haven: Yale University Press, 1940. Full study of Harington's translation of Ariosto, with discussion of his critical apparatus.

Schmutzler, Karl E. "Harington's Metrical Paraphrases of the Seven Penitential Psalms: Three Manuscript Versions." *Papers of the Bibliographical Society of America* 53 (1959):240–51. Discusses the manuscripts of Harington's paraphrases, and prints Psalms 38, 102, and 130 from British Library Egerton MS 2711, with variants from the other manuscripts.

Sigerist, Henry E. "An Elizabethan Poet's Contribution to Public Health: Sir John Harington and the Water Closet." *Bulletin of the History of Medicine* 13 (1943):229–43. Assesses the importance and limitations of Harington's invention.

Strachey, Lytton. *Portraits in Miniature and other Essays*. London: Chatto & Windus, 1931. Includes a brief, lively, and perceptive account of Harington.

Trotter, Margaret. "Harington's Fountain." *Modern Language Notes* 58 (1943):614–16. On Harington's changes to Ariosto's fountain in *Orlando*, Book 42, and noting the illustration of the fountain at Kelston in Collinson's *The History of Antiquities . . . of Somerset*.

———. Letter. *Times Literary Supplement*, 30 December 1944, p. 631. Malatesta as source for a section of Harington's "Briefe Apologie."

Whipple, T. K. *Martial and the English Epigram from Sir Thomas Wyatt to Ben Jonson*. University of California Publications in Modern Philology, vol. 10, no. 4. Berkeley: University of California Press, 1925. Discusses Harington's imitation of Martial in the epigrams.

Yoch, James J. "Architecture as Virtue: The Luminous Palace from Homeric Dream to Stuart Propaganda." *Studies in Philology* 75 (1978):403–

29. Discusses Harington's version of various palaces in *Orlando* in the context of the uses of architecture as an emblem of princely virtue by Chapman, Jonson, and Inigo Jones.

Index